Plays from the Third Eye

By Martin Cooper

Published by Shadrock Press

ISBN 978-0-9556915-0-8

Contents

Introduction

In September 1995, I enrolled on a 2-year course at Morley College in Lambeth, South London. I had no idea, at the time, that this simple, mundane act would change the way my life progressed for the next few years and introduce me to a group of people that I still feel privileged to have known and worked with. The course was run by Craig Snelling and, under his tutelage we were introduced to the subtle and complex craft of acting. Like any group of people, we came to this class with differing degrees of ability, but over our time there, Craig gave each one of us his full attention and developed us in ways which, I am sure, most of us could not have foreseen.

At the end of our 'introduction' to acting we left, in 1997, and went on to form the Third Eye Theatre Company. We were not alone. Before us, Craig's class had produced the Twice As Loud Theatre Company and after us, came the Fourth Wall Theatre Company.

Over the succeeding years, these companies, and the diverse individuals within them continued to grow, developing, with Craig's help, our acting, directing, writing and stagecraft. We put on many productions at fringe theatres such as The Landor in Clapham, the White Bear in Kennington, Theatro Technis in Camden and the Hens and Chickens in Islington. I don't have enough information to give an exact chronology and the number of people involved is far too great to list here. Suffice to say, it was a unique time, full of uniquely talented and creative people.

Martin Cooper, November 2007.

Illegible Alien was first performed by the Third Eye Theatre Company

At the White Bear Theatre, 138 Kennington Park Road, London SE11
24th February – 7th March 1998

Director: Diana Chappell

Cast:
Alien - Chai Chit Fatt
Phyllis - Grenita Vitte
Bob - Martin Cooper

Stage Management:
Chris Thomas
Sarah Craig

Lighting: Isobel Hancock

Sound: Rob Widdicombe

Illegible Alien

Blackout. Lights come up to reveal a dimly lit, shabby apartment in New York. It's on the 5th floor of a block. There is a bed or sofa. A man lies on it asleep. He is wearing a white vest and shorts or jeans and has stubble on his face. There is an alcove upstage left by the window which is shadowy. There is a radio next to the bed/sofa. There is a coffee table with cups, two bottles of water and a mobile phone.On the floor, next to the bed/sofa there are several video cassettes. The man's name is Bob Pels. There is a door downstage right.

Bob is snoring lightly. He restlessly turns in his sleep. A light momentarily flashes in the shaded alcove illuminating the wall redly. At the same time, a low throbbing noise is heard, which slowly dies away to nothing. Bob is still snoring.

Bob: Hmmmf [grunts, coughs, lifts his head, then lowers it to the pillow. Snores some more. Suddenly, wakes and sits up in bed.] Huh? [A form appears in the alcove and moves half into the light, though still not clearly visible. It is at least as tall as a 6ft Man.

Alien: Man?

Bob: Huh?

Alien: Man.

Bob: Who're you? What d'ya want?

Alien: Want.

Bob: How long have you been there?

Alien: Since beginning. Water.

Bob: What d'ya want? Listen. I don't want any trouble. Just take what you like. I'm insured. Just take whatever.

Alien: I want?

Bob: Yes, just take what you want. No trouble. Take it and go.

Alien: And go.

Bob: Yes, just go. Take and go.

Alien: Take.

Bob: What the hell is this? Who the hell are...[a neon light flashes on and illuminates the alien briefly] ... what... shit.. [he stares at the dark form, realising he isn't dreaming] For God's sake what are you? How long have you been here?

Alien: Since beginning. Water.

Bob: You're not, I mean you don't seem...human.

Alien: Human.

Bob: No. Not human. Not Human.

Alien: Not human.

Bob: You're from.... you're from..... where are you from?

Alien: Where are you from?

Bob: No. You. Where?

Alien: Coca Cola.

Bob: I don't have.... wait, wait.... you're trying to tell me something, right?

Alien: Trying. Coca Cola, Harley Davidson....... water.

Bob: What do you eat? Maybe I could fix...

Alien: From beginning. Water.

Bob: Beginning? What?

Alien: Beginning.

Bob: You're from up there [points out window, to sky] right? Why here? Why me?

Alien: Water.

Bob: You wanna see water? Sure, hey, look [leaps out of bed to and picks up two bottles of water. Alien moves back a pace]. Water....water....understand? [Alien doesn't take water, so Bob puts them down again]

Alien: Good water.

Bob: You speak....you speak English..... Oh Christ! I can't believe I said that! Hey! take me to your leader! Resistance is futile! [Alien moves forward a step] Hey! Just kidding!

Alien: Speak.

Bob: Listen, why don't you try next door, number 104, the Grunburgers, they talk all the time. Talk me to sleep. One time I was there with Phyllis. Drinks party, you know? And Rachel, his wife, she starts on about their vacation in Tahiti. I musta dropped off, cos I remember comin' to about two hours later and she was describin' the marble interior in the hotel lobby and how the doorman, Herb I think his name was, always winked at her. So... go there! They got plenty to say! Plenty.

Alien: Watch water.

Bob: We got water, man. We got lotsa water [points to bottles of water] Water. You want water? Not a problem. Take. Take water.

Alien: From the beginning.

Bob: Listen pal, just take the water if that's what you want. There's a whole reservoir upstate. They wouldn't miss..... shit this is difficult. Where'd you come from?

Alien:From the beginning.

Bob: Beginning of what? Hey! The newsboys'd make a meal of you. Ya wanna interview? Stay right there! Where's the phone? [sees a mobile phone on the coffee table, walks quietly, gingerly across the room, dials hurriedly, waits] Herald? Listen. You wanna first encounter story?.....No....E.T! Hey listen, I got one here, now. A thousand bucks and you get to meet......hello?......Oh come on!.......hello? [puts phone down and stands looking at alien] How'd you get in here? You beam in? Like the TV? You beam down?

Alien: King. Tell. Water.

Bob: King? No king, man. This is the U.S.... President. We........have........president.
Alien: Water.

Bob:Sure...sure...water. He's got water too. That...we all got plenty. You want? [alien produces a glass globe] Hey! You're not gonna hurt me? Look...I just...I was asleep. I go
back to sleep. You take water. go. Huh? How about it? [alien advances a couple of steps toward Bob, Bob steps to the side, hands up] No trouble. No trouble. You....take....water. Go. Go ahead! it's all yours. Take as much as you want. [key turns in lock. door opens. Phyllis enters. Alien puts globe away again.] Phyllis? Phyllis? Don't move! Don't make a sound! I know what I'm doin!

Phyllis: What the hell is that?

Bob: Phyllis. Go back out. Go eat. See a movie.
Phyllis: Is this a joke Bob? I'm sick of your jokes. Get me a beer and get that thing out of here!

Alien: Phyllis.

Phyllis: What're you tryin' to pull, Bob? Get me a beer and put that thing outside.

Bob: This isn't a joke, Phyllis.....that's an alien.

Phyllis: What d'ya take me for? Captain Kirk? Cut the crap and get me a beer. I've had it with you. This, I don't need. So just...

Alien: President. Water.

Phyllis: Bob? What's goin' down here? Who's the guest?

Bob: I've been tryin to tell you, Phyllis. This....this GUY is from space. Look at him. He ain't us, he talks, but he ain't US. Still think it's a joke?

Phyllis: I guess not. What's it want?

Bob: It keeps sayin' 'Water', so I guess that's what it wants.

Phyllis: So give it water and tell it to fuck off. I'm takin a shower.

Bob: [pleading] Phyllis!...Phyllis!

Phyllis: A shower, Bob. I get outta there, it's gone OK? [to alien] nice ta meet ya pal, but we're busy right now. [she picks up bottles of water and hands them to alien] There's the water, so gorge. Enjoy! OK? [she leaves the room to go for a shower]

Bob: Phyllis! Phyllis! [to alien] Listen pal, you've ruined my catnap, you come in here like it was your place or somethin', you wrecked a nice romantic night I was plannin' with Phyllis.... and I want you to know you've OVERSTAYED man. This ain't a hotel, so get back to the mothership and eat dirt, OK? Eat dirt. [Alien steps toward Bob] Hey! Hey! Can't you take a joke? What the hell? Have a beer. Chill out. Hey! David Letterman's on in a minute! We can order a pizza. The guy's a laugh a minute! You'll love it. Or........or........or...... look, I've got every episode of 'Star Trek the Next Generation' on Video. You'll feel right at home. Look. You sit down.... I mean....Can you sit? I don't see no joints or nothin, but listen, stand if you want to. [Goes over to TV and fumbles with videos] So.... what's it to be? There's Letterman, Star Trek..... OH HEY! YES! I got 'The Forbidden Planet'... 50s 'B' Movie, but I love it. That bit where the invisible alien monster runs into the force field. You'll love it. [Phyllis walks in]

Phyllis: Is that thing still here? Hey, Bob. Can you unhook me? [He unhooks her. She sees video] What's that?

Bob: 'The Forbidden Planet', I thought.

Phyllis: I ain't watchin that shit again. You always run out the room.

Bob: I don't.

Phyllis: I'm not arguin'. Look, you go ahead and watch kiddy films with your boyfriend. I'm goin' to bed early. [she walks out the room]

Bob: Phyllis! But Phyllis! [to alien] Now see what you done? NOW! NO VIDEOS! NO WATER! NOTHIN'! [goes to closet, opens it and takes out a broom goes over and prods alien with it] NOW GIT! YOU AIN'T WELCOME HERE! YOU'VE UPSET PHYLLIS, AND WHEN YOU UPSET PHYLLIS, YOU RILE ME!....SO GIT!..... GO ON!....... GIT. [alien steps back into shadowy alcove and disappears. There is a flash of light, then nothing]. Well. I showed that fucker. I showed him. [the TV is still on with the sound turned down, Bob goes over and turns it up. Sits on end of the bed. There's a news report on A female newscaster is speaking]

Newscaster: We're just getting reports of a huge tidal wave heading toward New York from the direction of the Hurricane Samson in Mid-Atlantic. Federal Authorities are warning people to stay at home and keep calm...]

Bob: Water............OH CHRIST!..........Water!
[Blackout]

Learning to Salivate was first performed by the Third Eye theatre company at
The White Bear Theatre, 138 Kennington Park Road, London SE11
16th March – 3rd April 1999

Director: Rob Widdicombe

Cast:
Atta - Richard Stone/Julia Collings
Sarin - Martin Cooper

(for the purposes of this production, the character of Atta was split in two and the lines divided between two actors. The director felt it would enhance the surreality of the play to have two interrogators)

Learning To Salivate

Characters: Atta: Could be a man or woman of almost any age over about 25.

Sarin: Could also be a man or woman.

ATTA: Do you believe in the primacy of commodity?

SARIN: What does it mean?

ATTA: You own a washing machine?

SARIN: Yes.

ATTA: Dishwasher?

SARIN: Planning to get one. Stephanie wants......

ATTA: Car?

SARIN: Renault Clio.

ATTA: You want more, though?

SARIN: Doesn't everyone?

ATTA: Have you ever been drawn to asceticism?

SARIN: Ass....

ATTA: the religious life.

SARIN: Oh....... no.

ATTA: Do you ever think about the ineffable?

SARIN: What's this got to do with.....

ATTA: Imponderables.... unanswerable questions.

SARIN: Such as?

ATTA: Why am I here? What happens after? Is anything real?

SARIN: Uh..... not really.

ATTA: Be more precise.

SARIN: I just..... well, it has occurred to me.

ATTA: When? How often? In which room of the house? Have you discussed it with anyone else?

SARIN: When I was...... younger.

ATTA: Does it affect you now? Are you efficient? Do woodlice live in your bathroom?

SARIN: It was....something temporary. Like frisbees.... x-ray glasses...... skateboards.

ATTA: What about divinity?
[Silence]

ATTA: The Godhead. The gulf between humanity and the divine. Do you know of Aquinas? Paul Tillich? Do you believe that human attributes and qualities are analogous to the divine, but different because not infinite?

SARIN: Are you asking me if I believe in God?

ATTA: Answer the question.

SARIN: I can't.

ATTA: Do you believe?

SARIN: Sometimes I..... that is...... no.

ATTA: No?

SARIN: No.

ATTA: Never?

SARIN: Never.

ATTA: Can you imagine what it would be like?

SARIN: To be God?

ATTA: To believe in God.

SARIN: My mother is a Jehovah's Witness. She says God is waiting for me.

ATTA: Heve you ever agreed with her?
[Silence]

ATTA: About her activities?

SARIN: The Jehovah stuff?

ATTA: Yes.

SARIN: I love my mother.

ATTA: Answer the question please.

SARIN: It's what she does, that's all.

ATTA: Are you influenced by metaphysics?

SARIN: Look...... I came here for....... I mean, I don't see the relevance.

ATTA: We're just being thorough, Mr Sarin.

SARIN: I'm just an ordinary person trying to make a living.

ATTA: What about your insignificance?

SARIN: That's not fair. I don't feel that I am. It's not something I think.

ATTA: All those galaxies. Stars. An entire universe wheeling. Sublime. Unlimited. Dark. In you. You one small part. Life from gas. Only nothing bigger. You don't feel insignificant?

SARIN: If you put it like that.

ATTA: Do <u>you</u> put it like that?

SARIN: You did.

ATTA: Psychology? Are you an independent being with inalienable rights, self consciousness and a soul or a lump, dull, corporeal and atomic?

SARIN: I don't know.

ATTA: Do you care?

SARIN: My mother says.....

ATTA: Do you care?

SARIN: I don't think I want to....

ATTA: This is being videotaped.

SARIN: No.

ATTA: No?

SARIN: No I don't care.

ATTA: Have you got experience?

SARIN: Of what? I've eaten doughnuts, been on a speedboat, told jokes, I've been to pottery classes, I take vitamin B, I've fallen in a river.

ATTA: There's no need to be flippant.

SARIN: I wasn't being flippant. I don't know what you're asking me.

ATTA: Are you naturally rebellious?

SARIN: I don't think so.

ATTA: Is that a no?

SARIN: Yes.

ATTA: Do you believe in Dialectical Opposition?

SARIN: I ought to go. This isn't what I expected.

ATTA: Social Darwinism? The Evolution of Societies? Is That a creed you follow?

SARIN: I want what everyone else wants.

ATTA: Which is?

SARIN: A family, a nice home, a comfortable, happy life.

ATTA: Are you sure?

SARIN: Absolutely.

ATTA: What about death?

SARIN: Death?

ATTA: Comes to us all.

SARIN: I'm interested in life.

ATTA: Scenario. A perfect stranger is being attacked in the street by a man with an idea...

SARIN: A man with an idea?

ATTA: A man with a knife. Attacked by an idea with a knife, would you: (a) Sacrifice yourself to save them, (b) Ignore the idea and walk past, (c) Call the police when you came to a telephone box?

SARIN: C.

ATTA: What about euthanasia?

SARIN: People should be allowed to die with dignity.

ATTA: Is suicide dignified?

SARIN: It isn't suicide.

ATTA: What is it then?

SARIN: Release from suffering.

ATTA: Is suffering a bad thing?

SARIN: Of course it is.

ATTA: Always?

SARIN: I think so.

ATTA: Not character building?

SARIN: Sometimes, I suppose.

ATTA: Does it enoble the spirit?

SARIN: It could. Like in the war. Mum says that people were different. Left their doors open. If your house was bombed, people would...... would....

ATTA: Would what?

SARIN: Rally round.

ATTA: [Writes something down] Rally round. Yes. Would you like to expand?

SARIN: People were..... a community. United by common suffering. Shared bread. That kind of thing.

ATTA: That's a good thing? People united. Is a good thing?

SARIN: Isn't it?

ATTA: I'm asking you.

SARIN: I'm not sure. Maybe. In certain circumstances.

ATTA: Fascism. Was that a good thing?

SARIN: The Nazis?

ATTA: The Nazis, Mussolini, The Spanish Civil War. They were good things?

SARIN: Not really.

ATTA: You can't say no?

SARIN: Yes.

ATTA: What about trade unions?

SARIN: They serve a purpose.

ATTA: do they serve your purpose?

SARIN: I haven't got a purpose.

ATTA: Have you read Das Kapital?

SARIN: I like Stephen King. I've read The Shining, Christine, The Stand.

ATTA: [interrupting] Marxism. Have you read about it?

SARIN: that's Communism, isn't it?

ATTA: Is that a good thing?

SARIN: Everyone knows it doesn't work. Look at Russia. That fell to pieces, didn't it?

ATTA: Do you believe in Jesus?

SARIN: Well, he existed, didn't he?

ATTA: Is he alive now?

SARIN: He died.

ATTA: Have you ever been motivated by altruism, or ever felt philanthropic?
[Silence]

ATTA: Do you put yourself and your family first? Before all others? Are you prepared to do whatever is necessary to make sure they're alright? Even if.....

SARIN: If what?

ATTA: Are you?

SARIN: Of course.

ATTA: Do you think about symbols, metaphors, allegories or any kind of deeper meaning to things?

SARIN: I can cook.Stephanie likes grilled Trout.

ATTA: Is there a collective unconscious?

SARIN: I have a credit card. Co-operative Bank.

ATTA: Could you be taught to salivate at the sound of a bell?

SARIN: I'm sorry?

ATTA: Are you open to new ideas?

SARIN: Yes.

ATTA: Have you ever had any?

SARIN: New ideas?

ATTA: Yes.

SARIN: I think of improvements. I believe in continuous improvement.

ATTA: How are you with change? Can you manage change?

SARIN: I'm very.... adaptable.. I'm always open to..... to.....

ATTA: New ideas?

SARIN: Yes. New ideas.

ATTA: Are You prone to infection?

SARIN: I think I'm immune.

ATTA: If I said "People should always agree with company policy" would you agree?

SARIN: What?

ATTA: Would you agree?

SARIN: I don't.... I mean, I'm not...

ATTA: WOULD YOU AGREE?

SARIN: I........

ATTA:: AGREE!

SARIN: [screaming] I AGREEEE!

ATTA: I was merely asking you if you think you're the right person for this job.

SARIN: Oh...... yes........ yes....... most definitely...... yes .... I can knit....... I've been to Barnsley .... My father .... my mother ..... who art in Lewisham, furrowed be thy brow.......... I'm good at knots ...... All my friends wear sensible shoes .... I can survive for days on cream crackers and water ..... I have a front loader at home, got rid of the twin tub........ Renault Clio....... Kellogg's corn flakes, Halifax.......Daily Mirror...... Chris De Burgh....... yes....... yes .... yes...... yes...... I believe in masticating food properly, chew each mouthful a hundred times, I use Sure anti-perspirant, helps me feel confident, I do feel very, I walk everywhere in a controlled and purposeful manner..... My favourite dogs are Yorkshire Terriers, I support Brighton and Hove Albion, I drink in moderation.... the road of excess leads to the palace of.... of.....of .... of course I can, I know I can, I know I can, I ....thought I could, I thought I could anything they can do I can do better, I can do anything better than them... there are reasons beyond the ken of wit for why we get no faster relief........ clears a stuffy nose effectively...relieves for up to 12 hours... I want to tape record my dreams.... yesterday I saw a partial eclipse.... occluded, occupant, occupational hazard........therapy... I've never had a single worried man written on my face in my day job, or a double Jamieson's in the evening as a nightcap.... a fix, I fix, he fixes, she fixes carburettors... and vending machines.... why only sixteen to a pack.... all those tablets... written on the tablets... the coefficient of all rational argument is pi times the radius of a dry tickly cough, take me, I'm yours, I never holiday near the San Andraes fault, intermittent fault, nobody's fault but my own, nobody. I am nobody, nobody at all, no, no, no, no, nobody whatsoever, If I stand still too long I quiver.... but nothing can receive incandescence like a parabolic negelector, for too long neglected, at school, Mrs Whidmer, at any time, night or best years of your long life, short knife, stanley, tile till toll, tuppence, birdseed, sang carols outside until they fed me, In a cage I was which resonated to the sounds of the four stroke cycle, ignition, exhaust, burnt out, made of frail stuff like humans are, or could be. Could be. At least could have been. I believe in it. There's no need to rinse me. I drip. I lose more moisture. Out into the dry volcanic exchange rate I go like a winged melon. I never could wish. No. Not for anything. I never even wished to wish. The pivot of a gamble is a wish. Otherwise flat. Otherwise, otherwise. Otherwise wise. can you help me. why only sixteen to a pack? why what? What? Why! When what I took to be in fact wasn't holy or even nice to the touch, I can live for days on cream crackers. I can do. I. I. I. I. I. I. I. I.

[lights slowly fade to blackout and the voice gets quieter and quieter until silent]

Mutually Exclusive was first performed by the Third Eye Theatre Company,
As part of the European Theatre and Arts Festival
at Theatro Technis, 26 Crowndale Road, Camden, London NW1
9th – 12th October 1997

Director: Francisco Paco Lara

Cast:
Julia - Gillian Kelly
Fred - Gerrard Fernandez

Mutually Exclusive

Julia and Fred have decided to take a vacation in New Hampshire. On their first day there, they decide to picnic under the stars.....

[blackout. Lights slowly come up to reveal a night time scene in the New Hampshire countryside. Fred and Julia are sitting on their coats in a field]

Julia: Fred? Do you think there are people on other stars?

Fred: Sure.

Julia: And thinking what we're thinking.... about people like us?

Fred: Sure.

Julia: I dreamt once that I was lookin' at the moon. Late at night it was, in my dream I mean, and I was lyin' in a grassy hill, with conifers higher up and I was lookin' up at the moon. The grass under me was wet, I remember that, and in my eyes the moon was big, like a grapefruit. Suddenly somethin' in me was like rushin' out, out, out, out. I was passin' through space an' everything seemed like a blur. I was reachin' with my mind. Reachin' for the moon. You ever have anythin' like that, Fred?

Fred: Sure.

Julia: Sometimes life seems like a mirage for me, Fred. It's like I'm here, but I'm not here, you know? Is there any Ice cream left Fred? Pass it over. Is there a spoon? Thanks. Yeah.... like I don't know whether I exist or not. Like my senses aren't real? Have you heard of Heidegger, Fred? He said the whole history of philosophy can be like condensed into one question. Can you believe that, Fred?

Fred: Sure.

Julia: Yes and you know what that question was Fred? Fred you've got your hand on my tit, please take it off.. and yeah, you know what that question was? It was 'What is being?' I just think that's so profound. I've been thinkin' about it a lot. Geraldine at the sushi bar says it was really I-mmanuel Kant actually. I hate the way she says 'actually' every second breath. It's like she's the fount of all wisdom or somethin'. Anyhow she didn't do the Introduction to Philosophy course, so I guess she wouldn't know, would she, Fred?

Fred: Nope.

Julia: So anyhow, my dad was sayin' I shouldn't waste my time with all this philosophy stuff, he says I oughtta think on gettin' fixed up with some guy, but I don't know if that's what I want. I've got a MIND Fred an' I'm just beginnin' to explore it. If I got hooked up now, well, I might be unfulfilled for the rest of my life. I heard about this guy who was a New York lawyer. He made big bucks, Fred. He was rich! And he jus' left it all to explore his psyche. He lives in this hut up in Alaska, an' exists by huntin' an' fishin'. Don't you think that's cool?

Fred: Uh huh.

Julia: Fred? When you're fixin' people's cars, do you ever like wonder what it's all for? Do you ever I mean look out the window and see that the people in the street are, like, shells, you know?

Fred: Sure.

Julia: No. You don't understand me. I mean that the consciousness I experience IS me. That there is no essential self and that what we think of as ourselves is just a pile of fragments, like cracked ice or somethin?

Fred: Uh huh.

Julia: I think that, Fred. I think like Hume did... David Hume, Scottish. What he said was "There is no thinker behind the thought". It was his Bunch Theory.... or Bundles. Do you ever feel the insubstantial nature of the thinker in you.. like it's not really there?

Fred: Nope. You got a cigarette?

Julia: Sure, Fred. Here.. [takes out a pack of cigarettes from her coat she's sitting on and hands it to Fred] I worry though, that we might be thinkin' too much an' not doin' enough. We live in a world where people suffer, Fred, REALLY suffer. Like, I mean, we think sufferin' is denting your fender or bitin' into a rotten apple, but the world is full of people who need love, help, healing. Who's there to help 'em out? Mother Teresa, that's who. There's not enough of her out there, Fred. Who knows when I might need her... or you, Fred? She's so .... saintly, you know? I wish I could be like her. She puts us all to shame, Fred. To shame. Fred.. where ya goin?

Fred: Get the portable from the car. Game's on later. You want corn chips? [exits to go to the car]

Julia: [calls after him] Can ya get my sweater, Fred? I'm feelin' a chill out here. So Fred, what d'ya think of Yoga, huh?

Fred: [shouts back from the car] Can't hear ya sweetheart.

Julia: I SAID YOGA. WHAT ABOUT IT?

Fred: No...... there's more Ice Cream...... want that?

Julia: NO, FRED, I......... oh skip it.
[brief silence. Julia lies back]

Julia: I was readin', Fred. About the Hubble Space Telescope? You know it sees back almost to the beginnin' of time. So, like,.... they've found these funny blotches in the sky that prove there was a big bang. You know the universe back then was no bigger than an atom? Like, WE was in there Fred. No more than one atom. Of course, it was all crushed together you know? I mean it was DENSE, Fred, REALLY DENSE. It was like.... well, you know in the scrapyard over on the east side, Fred? Where they compress those old cars? Well I was watchin' that the other day and I thought... the big bang was just like that.

Fred: Uh huh. [he picks up a plate, opens a box of crackers and starts spreading butter on them]

Julia: Only in reverse, Fred. Stuff was all comin' out all over the place. We were in there somewhere Fred, but it beats me where. I've spent a lot of time on this, Fred, and you know what I think?

Fred: [Eating a cheese cracker] Nope, what?

Julia: I think our SUBSTANCE was there... but not our FORM. It's like what Plato..... or Aristotle, I can't remember which, but one of 'em, said. everything is composed of substance in various forms. The forms are like mere passin' illusions, Fred, only the substance is real..... like the TV?

Fred: [shoves another cracker in his mouth] Yeah?

Julia: Yeah, like we think we see people an' stuff on TV, but all it is is little spots of light. Teensy little dots. Only we think it's not. We see all sortsa stuff, cars, buildings, people and it's really only little dots. Everythin's like that, Fred. We are merely ripples on the sea, Fred. Ripples. Fred... you know what SARTREZ said? JOHN PAUL SARTREZ?

Fred: Nope. What?

Julia: He said "The only freedom we have is the freedom to choose the manner of our own bondage".... doncha think that's a mindfuck Fred? I mean to think shit like that. I mean, he's so right. Look at marriage, Fred. I mean we all have to marry someone, don't we? HOLY WEDLOCK. Only Mary Lopez in the Raoul's Deli says somethin' different. [giggles] You know what she calls it, Fred, huh?
Fred: No. What?

Julia: She calls it holy padlock. FRED! [giggles] GEDDIT? HOLY PADLOCK. And I immediately thought of SARTREZ and I said to myself "Yes, Julia, that's entirely correct.... we have to choose between one padlock and another" only I guess we don't all the time, I mean some people don't get married at all. Right, Fred?

Fred: Sure.

Julia: Yeah.... but look at 'em, Fred. They're the loneliest people on God's Earth. That isn't ta say, Fred, that you can't be lonely AND married. You sure can. My mom was always alone. If dad wasn't workin' at the Alley he was out shootin' pool and drinkin' way too much. She was a lonely woman, Fred, an' she died that way, too. But.... but... on the other hand, there's that Clara Belmont who lives in that old house on Firtree and Lexington? She never married. And look at the way she shuffles from place to place and those pathetic little print dresses and flat shoes she wears. She looks so sad. And she never does nothin' to her hair. She's a hopeless case, I know, but it's the exception that proves the rule, Fred. And she sure is that.

Fred: [eating and apple] mmmm.

Julia: So.... what've you got? Lonely if you don't, lonely, maybe, if you do. But at least if you do it's only maybe. Not every marriage has perfect results. Take Martha, Fred? You know Martha Conroy? She makes those little souveneir moccassins they sell up top of Mt. Washington? You know, the one you can drive up. All six thousand feet? Well, she's had a lot of itching... well, you know where....

Fred: No.

Julia: Woman's place.. you know, her pussy.

Fred: Oh yeah.

Julia: So Doc Neisbaum, you know, the one with the Doberman and the Mercedes? Well he said that irritation in the pubic area was common in women of her age. OF HER AGE! She's only 29, for christ's sake! She's a month older than me! What does he mean 'of her age'? So he says she should use this fungicidal cream? FUNGICIDAL? What does he think, she's growin' MUSHROOMS or somethin? So she blames her husband for that. Turns out she was right. September comes around and she catches him an' Lynette Schneider in HER BED! Now... you tell me if Martha wouldn't have been better off not tyin' the knot in the first place. See what I mean? Holy Padlock, Fred. The manner of our own bondage. Sartrez. He knew what. [pause. Julia props herself on her elbows] Some're happy, Fred. Some are. But back there in the big bang, Fred, we was all squashed in together. But we didn't know it then of course. We didn't know it then.

Fred: Nope. D'ya bring any cheese? These crackers're a little dry.

Julia: There's a freezer box in the trunk. [Fred gets up and exits to the car. Julia calls after him] FRED?...........FRED? THERE'S

SOME MINTS IN THE GLOVE COMPARTMENT....... COULD YOU? [Fred returns with Freezer box]

Julia: You know, Fred? We're so suited, you and I. It's a joy to spend time with someone who you know you can share your secret self with, you know? You an' me... we got some deep stuff between us. You know that. I mean, conversations like this don't grow on trees, Fred. They're as rare as hen's teeth. In this be-knighted world, Fred, it's so precious to find someone you can enter into a true spiritual communion with. Ya know what I mean?

Fred: Sure.
[long silence. They both lay back and look at the sky]

Fred: Julia?

Julia: Yes, Fred, sweetie?

Fred: Ya want to screw now?
[lights fade to blackout]

Omega Time was first performed by the Fourth Wall Theatre Company
At the White Bear Theatre, 138 Kennington Park Road, London SE11
27th April – 15th May 1999.

Director: Tim Dodd

Cast:

God -	Anthony Bull
Assistant -	Michelle Greenidge
St. John -	Dennis Naughton
St. Michael -	Ian Jeffrey
Paparazzi -	Tyrone Atkins
	Dez Drummond
	Phil Jarvis
Masseuse -	Zoe Stevens
Manicurist -	Sona Vyas
Butler -	Dez Drummond

Omega Time

God: Gimme the details.

Assistant: Well....

God: Yes?

Assistant: Right. You sounded the last trumpet about...... about......

God: 18 hours.

Assistant: 18 hours ago, right?

God: Right.

Assistant: We had the four riders.

God: They all turned up?

Assistant: Yeah.... Pestilence, War, Death and er.......

God: What about Famine?

Assistant: Late.

God: Late?

Assistant: Yeah, the train, you know how it is, derailment at albuquerque.

God: What happened to his horse?

Assistant: Her horse.

God: Huh?

Assistant: Her. It's a she.

God: This is a mess. No-one told me about that.... Listen, can we start over?

Assistant: Well.... the last trumpet....

God: What about the last trumpet?

Assistant: Well.... it's not the second to last trumpet.... not penultimate, if you get me.

God: Who's makin the rules here, you or me?

Assistant: Oh, you, definitely you.

God: Let's get this straight. I'll have as many trumpets as it takes to get this thing right, OK? We gotta be fair. What's the deal on the last minute repentances?

Assistant: Well I jus got the standard deviation graph, statistical analysis an' all that stuff, they're right here [he shuffles a few papers] yeah right..... we got 55% of the upper quartile, 42% of...

God: Upper quartile?

Assistant: Social class A and B. You know. Read the New York Times, watch Seinfeld, eat Haagen Dasz.

God: What about drunks and hookers?

Assistant: Not so good. Not at last count.

God: lemme hear it.

Assistant: Well, it's demographically complex. Northern Europe, not so bad. Big cities we scored better. Lots of social deprivation, poverty, exclusion, livin' hand to mouth. You know the story. There we got a handsome 60% overall.

God: That's good?

Assistant: Better than him.

God: Any room for negotiation? Borderline cases?

Assistant: Well.... he's willing to talk.

God: What'd he say?

Assistant: Two C1 or C2's for every A or B.

God: Forget it.

Assistant: But...doncha think a worthy, well meaning, relatively naive buncha bums'd be good P.R.?

God: Not a chance. We're the upmarket outfit. He's pissin' in the wind. We need some class, I'm sick of all this meek inheriting the Earth stuff.

Assistant: It was you that said it.

God: I was havin' a bad day. Look. My fiscal arrangements require a good team of economically gifted individuals. We need a solid currency, low inflation etc.. etc.

Assistant: What about boardroom pay deals?

God: What about 'em? We pay the going rate. These guys gotta get adequate remuneration or they walk.

Assistant: Excuse me, but... well..... you don't seem yourself today.
God: Blame him.

Assistant: HIM!!!!????

God: Yeah, it's in the manifesto. We continue some of his policies for ... a while, because.... well...... they do seem to work, economically, that is.

Assistant: Not here! I mean....well..... I thought money was outta the picture. It mean bein' the root of all evil an' all?

God: We need some kinda credit system. This operation has associated costs. Plant and machinery needs to be amortised over time. We have to recoup that.

Assistant: But with money you get work.

God: Huh?

Assistant: Economic activity is based on the exchange of labour for pay, which sounds fine, but the owners of the methods of production have to make a profit.

God: So what? I'm the owner.

Assistant: Well... you'll need to pay people less than it costs to produce the goods or you're broke.
[silence]

Assistant: Look. It's like this. You add up raw material costs, administration, production, plant and machinery, servicing loans and whatever that comes to is your costs, right?

God: er... right.

Assistant: So pay is a part of that.

God: What're you gettin' at?

Assistant: You pay people less than the real value of their labours, or the business goes down.

God: Oh.

Assistant: There's good news. We got Keynes and Galbraith. It was touch and go, but....

God: That's great! What're our trade prospects?

Assistant: Well.... we need heat and light. There's plenty of heat down there, so the deal is we tap into that, and turn it into useable electricity with a feed up here.

God: And in return?

Assistant: We give them a pitifully inadequate air conditioning system that raises hopes initially but confirms their worst fears after cutover.

God: That doesn't sound fair.

Assistant: Have you forgotten? "Abandon hope all ye who enter here".

God: Oh... yeah. It did kinda slip my mind.Who're the shareholders?

Assistant: [chuckling] They are.

God: Who are?

Assistant: the damned. They couldn't take it with them, so they signed agreements that their earthly wealth is converted to shares in Paradise inc. with dividends.

God: Dividends?

Assistant: Every 10,000 years, each of them gets a single drop of water squeezed onto their tongue from a sponge.

God: What about him?
Assistant: He gets a seat on the board, a Mercedes and expenses.

God: I don't know.....

Assistant: He'll throw in some accountants. So far he's got all of them.

God: ALL????

Assistant: All.

God: But we can't operate without....

Assistant: that's why this deal makes sense.

God: J.C. won't like it.

Assistant: He doesn't have your authority and kudos.

God: I thought he did.

Assistant: Not according to the latest polls.

God: Couldn't we make it 5,000?

Assistant: Huh?

God: A drop of water every 5,000 years. It'd be, well, kinder.

Assistant: Not without overheating the economy. It'd increase the PSBR above acceptable limits. There'd be a monetary squeeze. Maybe even a mead ration.

God: That's out of the question.

Assistant: We could pitch a few of the dissidents into the lake of fire.

God: Who're you thinkin' of?

Assistant: The 'repatriate the damned' movement. You know, the bleeding heart liberals. We could start with Julian of Norwich.

God: But she's highly regarded.

Assistant: Not a saint though.

God: Isn't she? I thought...

Assistant: Nope. No canonisation contract. I checked. Short term performance monitoring.

God: That's great!

Assistant: Isn't it.

God: Whose idea was that?

Assistant: Well.... in all modesty....

God: You??

Assistant: I'm not just a pretty face.

God: But what about the ethics committee?

Assistant: Pitch them in as well, the lake needs stoking anyhow.

God: That's not easy to achieve. I mean, it could be construed by the assembly of saints as an impeachable offense.

Assistant: Ahhhh c'mon. Give them a raise. They'll sit easy with that.

God: 10% be enough?

Assistant: 5% would be better. We need to think about the next spending round. There's maintenance and upkeep to think about.

God: Such as?

Assistant: Education. We need to keep classes down to 30 cherubs or less. Transport. Wing repair costs are through the roof.Then there's social welfare.

God: Uh huh?

Assistant: Yeah. Day care centres for decrepit saints, medication programmes to deal with ambrosia addiction. Then there's purgatory.

God: I forgot about that.

Assistant: Yeah. Think about it. The whole place thermostatically controlled. It has to be hotter than pleasant but cooler than torment at all times. It's in the contract. To do that, we need lots of expensive electronics, computer systems and skilled staff to run them.... and there's a shortage.

God: Oh?

Assistant: We're not doin' so well in that sector. He got most of the best analysts. Computers bein' the devil's tool an' all that.

God: True. So what do we do?

Assistant: I've introduced a two-prong approach. We start up a sabbatical programme. People tired of singin' hymns and constant adoration get a free hellfire break. All expenses paid. At the same time we recruit temporary workers with the requisite skills. They get a holiday from eternal damnation - and they work for nothin'! Great isn't it?
[There's a loud buzz] [Assistant leans over and picks up an entryphone]

Assistant: Shit! It's St. John.

God: What'll we say?

Assistant: What am I? My brother's keeper?

God: What does he want?

Assistant: Search me.

God: OK. Let him in.
[A presses a button. John enters]

John: Gracious Lord.

God: What is it? Can't ya see I'm busy?

John: I know, lord, but, well.... some of the others are getting restive. I have, just this minute, seen brother Thomas banging his head with a melon.

God: Is he paid to do that?

Assistant: Not according to his contract of employment.

John: Morale is low, my Lord.

God: What is it this time?

John: The workload, oh Lord.

God: I can't expect loyalty? I'm paying you enough for God's sake.

John: Teresa and Augustine between them have worked an 18 hour stretch. I myself have processed Austria, Chile and Glamorgan.

God: What d'ya want, a medal?

John: A break would be nice.

God: A BREAK?!!! This is the last judgement, dammit.

John: I know, Lord, but accuracy is suffering. Only five minutes ago, Adolf Hitler was admitted through a clerical error.

God: We do need a military adviser.

John: But even so......

God: Is that all?

John: Sorry?

God: If that's all you came to tell me, then you can get back to work.

John: But......

God: Get. And don't waste my time.

John: Yes, Lord
[John exits]

Assistant: So what do we do about the Jews?

God: The Jews?

Assistant: Yeah. Due to a group responsibility clause, they are jointly and severally culpable for the crucifixion.

God: That can't be!

Assistant: It's true. I assure you. I checked it out myself.

God: Have they gone yet?

Assistant: They're waiting for the elevator.

God: Get them back.

Assistant: What about the Golden Calf episode? You expressly said no false idols.

God: We gotta be pragmatic don't we? That was then and this is now. How we gonna operate the machinery of state without 'em? Cut it out. they're in.

Assistant: Whatever you say.

God: Damn right. Let's get this straight. We need the skills. Anyone, I mean ANYONE with business, industrial, military or political knowledge is in.

Assistant: The retail sector?

God: Them too. Who's that leave?

Assistant: Well.... there's the Arts. Ballet dancers, poets, actors, directors.... all that shit.

God: They can all go.

Assistant: But there're some good people there.

God: They're out. Money management does not require intuitive thinking.

Assistant: But even so.... what about Peter Hall, Richard Attenborough? Then there's Peter Greenaway, Stockhausen, The Spice Girls!

God: Alright, alright. Purgatory. A thousand years we review the situation. I ain't got time for this. Where's the seventh seal?

Assistant: cutbacks. Those seals are solid platinum. At the end of the financial review we only had money for 6 and a half. We got 6 good quality seals and.......

God: And what?

Assistant: A plastic dustbin lid. But it works! We've tested it.

God: I do not want to be known as a cheapskate.

Assistant: It's OK, we've painted it. It looks like platinum. It'll be OK. I mean, these seals...... its useless expense if you ask me. They'll never be used again.

God: It looks bad. My image.

Assistant: We've told the press it's a technical innovation. A lightweight platinum substitute.

God: they bought it?

Assistant: So far.

God: Keep me informed.

Assistant: I'm on it, Lord.

[Enter St Michael]

God: Michael!!! Good to see ya. What can I do for you!!!

Michael: Don't try ta weasel out of it! What happened about the textile franchise?

God: I don't know what you mean. Michael, I think....

Michael: Don't play the innocent. I heard you put it out to tender.

God: Yeah? So what if I did?

Michael: Me an' the boys've worked real hard on this.

God: You're breakin' my heart.

Michael: I thought we had a deal.

God: Yeah. Don't think so much. You're paid. That's all you need to think about.

Michael: But why????

God: I got a better offer.

Michael: What about my expenditure? I got a dozen guys out there sweatin' over the Autumn collection. You oughtta see this stuff. Cheesy. You'll love the uniform for the ladies. These neat light blue coulottes that go to the knee. Lightweight cotton. Seductive white silk blouse with optional wing holes, patent blue court shoes, tasteful angora scarf with a choice of ecumenical patterns...

God: Forget it.

Michael: Who was it?

God: Who was who?

Michael: Who muscled in?

God: Work it out for yourself.

Michael: Gimme a clue at least.

God: OK. Hooves.

Michael: This is a joke ain't it?

God: Yeah. And you're the punchline.

Michael: It'll be substandard. Bad stitching. Uneven hems. Cheap material. It needs good people to make this stuff.

God: They're all down there and available to do piece work for peanuts.

Michael: It's cheap labour. That's unfair business practice!

God: Get me a violin.

Michael: You'll come crawling back. You wait and see!

[Michael exits]

[Turns to his assistant]
God: So how we doin'?

[Assistant looks a the computer screen and punches a few keys]

Assistant: Shit.

God: What is it?

Assistant: There's been an administrative mix-up. The computer went down and they were checking people in manually. We didn't get the procedures worked out in advance.

God: And what?

Assistant: And..... so far, two billion've been consigned to the flames without any assessment, CV checks or sin counts.

God: FOR FUCK'S SAKE! DO I NEED TO DO EVERYTHING MYSELF???!!! OK! REWIND. BACK TO SCRATCH. BACK OUT THE DATABASE AND START AGAIN! GO FIND MY TRUMPET.

Assistant: But the extra cost....

God: GET MY FUCKIN' TRUMPET. NOW!!!!!

[Assistant rushes out and G sits shaking his head, a look of disbelief on his face. Fade, slowly, to black]

One Axe Play was performed by the Fourth Wall Theatre Company
at the White Bear Theatre, 138 Kennington Park Road, London SE11
27th April – 15th May 1999.

Directors: Sona Vyas and Toby Wicks

Cast:
Brad - Phil Jarvis
Laurie - Sally Fensome
Michael - Tyrone Atkins

One Axe Play

It's about nine o'clock at night in Central Park, New York. Brad and Laurie sit on the grass looking at the sky. There is the sound of distant traffic.

Laurie: It's sure beautiful, Brad, isn't it?

Brad: What is?

Laurie: The grass, the moon, the stars. And I can see it all reflected in your eyes.

Brad: You can?

Laurie: Sure! There it all is. Right in there. [she points at his head with her index finger]... Brad....?

Brad: Huh?

Laurie: Brad! Are you listenin' to me? You should, you know, listen. It shows a lack of respect.

Brad: You know I respect you honey.... in fact.....[pause]

Laurie: What, Brad? In fact...what?

Brad: Er....

Laurie: Brad! Have you got somethin' to say or haven't you? You weren't so shy when you was kissin' me jus' now. [pause] So.... Brad.... What have you got that you want me to know?

Brad: Well, Laurie, honey, I was talkin' to Mom the other day. She was tellin' me how happy her and Dad've been all these years and how it's been her joy to raise such good kids.

Laurie: She's very proud of you, Brad. She told me as much.
[Enter Michael, stage right, carrying an axe]

Brad: [suddenly worried, because he sees Michael] Laurie...... Laurie....

Laurie: [Irritated] What Brad..... what?
[Michael is a few feet away from them now. He stops, feet apart, holding the axe in front of him and glares at them. Brad and Laurie just stare at him]

Brad: Er... hi!

Laurie:[quietly] Brad. Get up slowly. Let's just go. He looks like trouble.

Michael: No you don't. You sit right there.

Brad: Or what?

Laurie: Yes. Or what?

Michael: Or I use this.
[silence for a minute. Every time Brad or Laurie move a little, Michael shifts his stance and raises the axe again]

Michael: What're you doin' in my park?

Laurie: We were.... YOUR park?

Michael: It's mine. I bought it.

Brad: BOUGHT Central Park? That's impossible.

Michael: I've got a receipt. This is my kingdom. Here... I'M the law.

Laurie: [to Brad] Brad, he's out to lunch. He's gonna kill us.....

Brad: Quiet, honey, I'm thinkin'.

Michael: What you thinkin' about bro? You plannin' somethin'?

Brad: Me? No.

Laurie: Brad! You call yourself a man? He's just some simp. Brad! You get me home! NOW!

Brad: Laurie, it's not that simple. He has an axe.

Laurie: You think he'll use it? [looks pointedly at Michael] He hasn't got the guts! Now... take me home, Brad. I'm cold.

Brad: We don't know that, Laurie. I'll just ask him....

Laurie: You'll ask him NOTHIN'.. you understand? WE'RE GOIN! NOW! NOW GET UP AND WALK, BRAD! LIKE A MAN!

Michael: You sit there, lady, or you get stomped.

Brad: Stomped?

Michael: You get what you should, accordin' to the law.

Laurie: Whose law, buster? The law don't like guys like you carryin' an axe.

Michael: I was jus' choppin' wood when I saw you.

Brad: At night? You was choppin' wood at night?

Michael: The best time.

Brad: How'd you figure that?

Michael: The blade gets cold. Makes it sharper.

Brad: Bullshit! The blade's as sharp as it is. The heat don't count.

Michael: That's all you know. This my best axe. It gets cold, it gets sharp.

Laurie: Brad... don't listen to him.... he's a yoyo.

Brad: Laurie... I don't think you should speak so loud... he might....

Michael: I heard, pal. I heard. What's she? Some lush you picked up? She looks like a lush.

Brad: You don't talk about her like that, OK? Laurie, honey, I'm sorry.... I'm sorry we got into this... but I'm gonna get us out, OK?

Michael: And how you gonna do that, fat boy? Who's got the axe?

Brad: I'm not fat.

Michael: Figure of speech. Don't you understand metaphors?

Brad: Sure, I understand.... but that wasn't a...

Michael:You got the time?

Laurie: Sure... it's...... nine........eighteen.

Michael: Late..... it's late.

Brad: You gotta be somewhere?

Michael: Nothin' pressin'. I was just askin' that's all.

Brad: Can we go? It's cold.

Michael: What'll I do with this axe?

Brad: Chop wood. You got more wood, don't you?

Michael: Nope.

Brad: No more wood? What about all those trees?

Michael: Park regulations. No cuttin' at trees.

Brad: I thought you was king?

Michael: I'm king, but I don't make the tree rules here.

Brad: What kind of king is that?

Michael: A spiritual king. A king of the heart. A forester king.

Brad: Uh huh? [looks at Laurie]
[long pause]

Michael: One hundred and eighty six thousand! [He looks up at the sky. Brad and Laurie look at each other, but remain silent]

Michael: 186,000 miles per second. Light. It goes that fast! If you was on a planet out in space a long way, with a super big telescope, you'd see Adolf Hitler.... Julius Caesar.... Dinosaurs even....

Brad: Oh..... sure..... that's right..... isn't it Laurie?

Laurie: Don't ask me, Brad. I thought I was with a man.

Brad: When? Who?

Laurie: YOU, STUPID! What're you goin' to do about him?

Michael: You keep your mouth shut, lady. Hey... you're a sweet little thing. pity about the mouth you got.

Brad: Listen, man, we don't want no..... I mean I don't want to fight you.

Michael: You? Fight me? That's good. worth a belly laugh, for sure. You even try to get up, I'll have your head off. Off with your head! ha! ha! Off with his head!

Brad: Why.... would you want to do that?

Michael: I'm a king. That's what kings do.

Brad: Listen.... [he digs in his pocket]

Michael: Careful, fat boy, nothin' sudden, that'd be silly.

Brad: Listen, here's ten bucks. Ten bucks and you let us go.

Michael: That's a bribe!

Brad: Look on it as a gift.

Michael: No strings?

Brad: No strings.

Michael: OK. I'll take it.[he snatches the money]

Brad: So......?

Michael: So what?

Brad: Can we go?

Michael: Nope.

Brad: the money...... I thought.....

Michael: Well you thought wrong. You said it was a gift.

Brad: Well....yes, it was a gift, but I thought you'd be kind enough to.....

Michael: That was kinda silly wasn't it? Anyone could see I'm nuts.I can't remember no gift, anyhow.
Brad: I just gave it you.

Michael: I've got a short attention span. My schoolin' suffered for it. That's how I wound up king here.

Brad: Look... I'm sorry you've had a hard time of it, but.....

Michael: Hard time? You don't know. You couldn't possibly know.

Brad: I didn't mean to presume...

Michael: That's right. I'll do all the presumin' here. Sit down.

Laurie: We ARE sitting down.

Michael: So lie down! Go on! Get down!

Laurie: The grass is wet, SIMP!

Michael: Are you gonna fix her mouth, or shall I?

Brad: You touch her and I'll.......I'll......

Laurie: Go on, Brad, what'll you do?...... nothin'....... NOTHIN...... that's what you'll do! [she sobs] .... To think, I seriously thought about gettin'.....[more sobs]

Michael: What you want with old gutless here? I'm here for you baby!.... Michael...... I've got a big, big axe! heh, heh.

Brad: Why you foul mouthed.....

Michael: What's wrong, Braddy boy... I was only talkin about my axe. You wanna make somethin' of it, huh? [grits his teeth and smiles insanely]

Brad: Look.... just let us go. I promise we won't say nothin'....

Laurie: Well you might not Brad, but I'm sure gonna tell everyone what a cowardly little shrimp you are. Why.... even Michael here's got more masculinity in his...... his....

Michael: My axe...

Laurie: In his....TOE.... than you ever got within a mile of...

Michael: You listen to her, Braddy boy, she's finally talkin' sense.
Laurie: Shush Michael.

Brad: What's with this 'Michael'? Who's he? Your new fiance'?

Michael: You shut your mouth, Braddy boy. She's with me now. You're history, pal. Ain't that so, lady? We'll be goin' now, but before that, how'd you like to get friendly with my axe? I know he likes you. heh, heh [insane grin]

Laurie: Shut up, Michael, I'm talkin.

Michael: She sure breathes fire, don't she? Lady, you're drillin holes in me.

Laurie: Listen, Michael, I'd like to go get a closer look at those trees over there.

Michael: Sure, honey, how close you wanna get?

Laurie: Close.

Brad: Laurie, Honey!

Laurie: So.... let's go!

Michael: Well, there's an offer. What's in it for you?

Laurie: I'd like to see what it's like to be with a real man.[gets up]

Michael: What about him?

Laurie: Him?.... Who cares..... he'll probably wait here for me...... or go DROWN IN THE SEWER! Who cares?

Brad: Laurie..... I......
[she takes Michael by the hand and they exit]

Brad: [Crying after her] I only wanted us to get out safe........ I thought you loved me Laurie......... I thought we was........ well....you got yourself into this...... [shouts] DON'T EXPECT TO FIND ME HERE WHEN YOU GET BACK!

LAURIE!.............LAURIE!...... CAN YOU HEAR ME?........ [louder still] LAURIE! [Laurie enters behind him, she has a bloodstained axe in her hands] LAUR......

Laurie: I'm here Brad.

Brad:[sees axe] What's that, Laurie? WHAT THE HELL IS THAT?

Laurie: It's an axe, Brad.
[Blackout]

Plenty of Space was first performed by the Fourth Wall Theatre Company
At the White Bear Theatre, 138 Kennington Park Road, London SE11
3rd – 14th November 1998

Director: Anthony Bull

Cast:
Emma - Sona Vyas
Carla - Sally Fensome
Ed - Jon Howard
Matt - Toby Wicks
Hester - Susanna Bas

Plenty Of Space

Lights come up on a living room in the home of Ed and Carla Strube. Centre stage is a sofa and a coffee table. A TV stage right with a plant on it. Backstage centre is a door that leads out.

Emma: Where does it go?

Carla: Huh?

Emma: IT. Where does it go?

Carla: We're not sure yet. Ed thinks Mars.

Emma: Where is Ed?

Carla: He's out there now.

Emma: Is is safe.... I mean can he breathe?

Carla: Well, he stuck his head through on Sunday and looked kinda blue when he popped back out, so we bought a dry suit and some aqualungs from 'Scuba City'.... you know [sings] 'Dive in and spear a deal, Scuba City it's a steal'

Emma: I hate that ad... it's so..... kitsch. That little guy dressed like a Barracuda......?

Carla: Yeah, so he tried it with that and it was ..... ok... and I checked in Reader's Digest, and it says "Mars has a thin atmosphere, low in Oxygen", so Ed figured, well, get breathing gear, wrap up warm and take the plunge. He's been out there every night since the weekend. Want some bagels and coffee?

Emma: Thank you, coffee'd be fine. Any doughnuts?
[Carla goes out to the kitchen. A pause. Emma picks up a magazine and flicks through it]

Emma: [shouts out to Carla] DO AQUALUNGS LAST THAT LONG?
[Carla returns with a tray full of cups, plates, coffee]

Carla: Well, you ain't heard the rest... so... anyhow, there he was, steppin' out in rubber gear and air bottles when Buster jumps through.

Emma: YOU LET BUSTER OUT THERE?

Carla: No, he just kinda jumped.

Emma: Uh huh.

Carla: yeah, and well I just kinda shrieked. I said BUSTER! YOU GET BACK HERE THIS MINUTE! Which was kinda silly because if there ain't no air then he wouldn't hear nothin' besides which he'd be dead in seconds. So Ed, he.....

Emma: OH GOD! What happened?
Carla: That's what I'm tellin ya.... Ed yells, DON'T WORRY BUSTER.... DADDY'S COMIN, and jumps through without a thought for his own safety, you know?

Emma: That was brave.

Carla: Sure... so I waited an' waited. Then I had, like, this brainwave you know. I ran upstairs an' found that toy periscope that Marcia bought the kids on Thanksgiving? I sorta poked it through and positioned it at a kind of angle, and there was Ed throwin rocks for Buster.

Emma: I guess it must be safe, huh? [pause] So... what're you doin fer Easter? Tony and the kids are comin' up from Massachusetts. You wanna drop by?

Carla: Sure, if I can drag Ed away from outer space.

Emma: Have you told anyone else about this Carla? You know, NASA, the Federal Agencies or anyone?

Carla: Well, Ed wanted to keep it quiet, you know how he gets......

Emma: So.....

Carla: Well, I managed to convince him that this ain't a toy, that we need to know if it's dangerous.... I mean there's the kids to think about... and like that we needed expert advice. So we got some head from the space agency comin this afternoon.

Emma: TODAY? Will it be on TV..... OH GOD..... LOOK AT MY HAIR!
Carla: Eat your bagels... your hair's fine.

Emma:When you called them, they thought you were a fruit, right?

Carla: Well, Ed called them up on Tuesday, you know their number? 800-1212-SPACE? well.. he had to redial 17 times before anyone'd even talk to him. Guess they never had this happen before.

Emma: Guess not. Can I go see?

Carla: Sure, it's out back, in the yard. Could you remind Ed that I exist while you're there?

Emma: Oh.... I don't know... I ain't goin through... I just thought.....

Carla: Oh Emma, just stick your head out... it's OK really.
[Emma exits. Carla exits briefly and comes back with bags of potato chips and a bowl of pistachios]

Carla: [shouts] YOU OK OUT THERE, EMMA?

Emma: [shouts from offstage] SURE. HEY, WHY'S IT FLASH SO?

Carla: [shouts back] NO IDEA. PRETTY THOUGH, AIN'T IT?
[Emma enters and sits on the sofa, next to Carla]

Emma: It sure is..... reminds me of my bathroom suite.
Carla: Oh..... yeah...

Emma: Same shade of blue.

Carla: To be perfectly frank, Emma, I'm gettin' tired of the whole thing. When the kids are around someone has to be there the whole time to make sure they don't go in.

Emma: Out.

Carla: Huh?

Emma: I guess it'd be out... you know, SPACE?

Carla: Oh, sure. Emma, could you do me a big favour?

Emma: Sure honey, name it.

Carla: Could you sit with it while I go down town..... the kids.....

Emma: Sure. The way it kinda hangs there.... spooky, ain't it? what about Ed?

Carla: He's ok. He's taken a thermometer and some bathroom scales with him this time. He calls it scientific experimentation... I've got another name for it...

Emma: Yeah?

Carla: Sex deprivation, Emma. If this goes on, I'm suing for divorce and custody.
[Emma laughs, Carla frowns]

Emma: Why'd you do that?

Carla: What?

Emma: Move your foot around like that?

Carla: I guess it happens when I'm angry.

Emma: You mad at Ed?

Carla: I'm gettin' there, honey. You know what he did today.... well, when I say today, I mean like 4:30 A.M.? He comes stridin' into our room.... OUR ROOM... carryin a huge lumpa rock. "Mars stone" he says. I just screamed "GET IT OUT"!
[Emma laughs. Carla starts twirling here foot rapidly]
[|Ed enters wearing fur coat and goggles, padded trousers and moon boots]

Ed: YO!

Emma: Where ya been Super hero?

Ed: She told you?

Emma: Sure. I jus' saw it myself.

Ed: Great isn't it? Buster loves it.

Emma: Should you be takin buster out there? I mean, I know the Russkies had dogs in space an' all, but, well, I mean, Buster..... he's kinda human.

Ed: Oh come on. You should be proud. Buster an' I have taken yet another giant leap for mankind.

Emma: Buster's a dog.

Carla: He bought a huge star spangled banner yesterday. It's out there now. Proclaiming the arrival of life, liberty and the American dream to a bunch of martian rocks. He even took his bugle.

Emma: So it is Mars, huh?

Ed: We don't know that. I checked for Orion, The Big Dipper, stuff like that. Couldn't see nothin'

Emma: Oh..... sure...... what I'd do too.[to Carla] Is he still..... you know...... compos mentis?

Ed: Look, Emma..... it ain't nuts. When you look up at the sky, right? You'd see the constellations, OK? With me so far?

Emma: So what?

Ed:If we was on Mars now, we'd see the same thing. Any planet herabouts you'd see Orion. I figured, well, check for that and I'd know I was still in the Solar System. I mean, hell, it could be anywhere out there. Anywhere. So don't get at me alright? I know what I'm doin.

Carla: OK, Ed, that'll do. Why don't you go see where Buster is?

Ed: It was my discovery. I saw it first.

Carla: I know you did, sweetheart. Now go check out Buster.

Ed: Buster's fine. I left him pissing against a rock.

Emma: Ed.... I really don't think.... I mean, he's only a dog.... you shouldn't leave him out there on his own..... he don't know Orion from a can of big and chunky.

Ed: You think I don't know my own dog, goddammit! Buster is perfectly OK. But I'm not so sure about you two.
[Ed turns and strides out of the room]

Emma: ED! I DIDN'T MEAN NOTHIN BY IT! I WAS JUST SAYIN', THAT'S ALL!

Carla: It's OK, Emma, this is what I get all the time now. One schoolboy tantrum after another.

Emma: They just don't grow up, do they? Carla, I'm thinkin' of redecorating. Whaddya think of the New England style? Kind of simple, but tasteful. I was lookin' at photographs in New England Homes and I saw just the interior. I mean, bigger than our place, and it had a basement. I always wanted a basement utility room..... you know, washer, dryer, boiler.... all stashed away, hidden from view, but with easy access. Somewhere to put pressed mango preserve.

Carla: Whatever, Emma, whatever.

Emma: Carla, honey, you OK? It's got you rattled, hasn't it?

Carla: Ever since that..... that THING appeared in our yard this place has been a complete madhouse, Emma. I don't live in a home anymore, it's like a launchpad..... Cape fucking Canaveral. [She starts to sob and Emma goes to her and hugs her] I'm a space widow. He loves that floating blue hoop out there more than me! [She sobs. The doorbell rings]

Emma: I'll get it. You just rest, hunn.
[Emma exits to answer the door. Carla just stares into space, demoralised. A few seconds later, Emma returns. She hesitantly steps into the living room and just looks at Carla.]

Emma: Carla.... er...... I think you should step out here a moment.... I mean..... er
[Matt Shadrock, A tall man wearing dark glasses and a grey suit walks in, followed by Hester Dimmock, a small woman in overalls, carrying a black suitcase.]

Matt: OK. Nobody move. The house is cordoned off. Federal quarentine laws are in force. We got a ring of state troopers and armoured personnel carriers outside. I'm declaring a local state of emergency.

Carla: Who the hell are you? Get outta my house NOW, or I call the cops. [She gets up. Stares at him defiantly. Matt pulls out an ID card]

Matt: Matt Shadrock, FBISA.

Emma: FBISA?

Matt: Federal Bureau for the Investigation of Space Anomalies.

Emma: I never heard of that.

Carla: Me neither.

Matt: You questionin' my authority? I could get this house bulldozed just like that [he clicks his fingers] so you just watch your attitude, lady. [At this point, Hester opens the suitcase and pulls out a black gadget, like a Geiger counter or a metal detector and begins to sweep it around the room, pointing it at things.]

Carla: What's she doin'? Tell her to put that away!

Matt: Just a precaution, Mrs.... er

Carla: Strube.

Matt: Mrs Strube. We have to establish a safe zone.

Emma: A safe zone.

Matt: Radioactivity, space viruses, the threat of terrestrial contamination. I'd appreciate you co-operation on this. We need to take a few readings.

Carla: [Freaking out] READINGS? WHAT KINDA READINGS?

Matt: Nothing to be alarmed about, Mrs Strube, Gamma Ray levels, X-Ray spectrographic analysis, Gravimetric sensing, neutrino intensity, high energy Proton scintillation counters. The usual stuff. If you don't mind, we'll be moving our equipment in right away. Can you take me to the anomaly?

Carla: Huh?

Emma: I think he means [she points out back]

Matt: It's out there?

Emma: Out there.

Matt: [to his assistant] Hester? It's out back.

Emma: [To Carla] Hester? [She starts to laugh. Matt and Hester exit]

Carla: This is gettin' too much, Emma. I wanna go to my mom's. You think they'll let me out?

Emma: There's state police outside, Carla. I don't think....... and anyhow, there's Ed and the kids. THE KIDS! Carla..... where, where....

Carla: Upstairs, on the Playstation. I got Ridge Racer for Rory's birthday present. They've been squabbling over it day and night. [pause] Emma, what'm I going to do? They're gonna turn this place into a laboratory. I don't wanna be a white mouse.

Emma: Cool down, honey. I'm here too, remember. I guess I won't be going anywhere, like, er.. home for example.

Carla: Oh, Emma, darling, I'm sorry!
[Emma shrugs, Matt re-enters]

Matt: Can you give me the precise location of your filial co-habitees?
[uncomprehending silence]

Emma: I think he means Ed and the kids.

Carla: Kids upstairs, Ed....... Ed.....

Matt: Where is Ed? [Silence. He strides over to Carla, grabs her by the shoulders.] Mrs Strube, your husband could be in grave danger. This is an issue of national security. I ask you again. WHERE IS HE?

Carla: [whimpering] He went in.

Emma: In? IN WHERE? Mrs Strube, I urge you to co-operate. The penalty for treasonous and unregulated harbouring of extraterrestrial phenomena is at least 75 years in the state correctional facility.

Emma: She is co-operating, dammit! Just let her speak, for God's sake! Look, it's simple. He's taking the dog for a walk....... on another planet.

[fade to blackout. Lights come up on Emma and Carla, sitting in the living room. They have cups of coffee]

Carla: What d'ya suppose they're doing out there, huh? Nobody tells me anything. I mean, whose house is this, anyway? [pause] And another thing. I never seen so much hardware as the stuff they took out back. I guess they gotta measure stuff, but did they need to bring mission control?

Emma: Carla.... I......

Carla: And you. Fat lotta good you were. You open the frigging door and in comes Arnold Shwarzenegger. We got a dozen SWAT teams outside and you lay out the red carpet [sarcastically] "Come on in, guys. You want a glass of Chardonnay?".
Emma: It wasn't like that.

Carla: Oh And what was it like, Emma? What was it like? [There's a loud buzzing noise, followed by an explosion from outside] What the fuck are they doing out there? This is 1984 re-enacted. Big fucking daddy. That's the reality here.

Emma: Brother.

Carla: What?

Emma: Brother. It was Big Brother. [Another loud noise from outside]
[Matt re-enters. Carla stands up, ready for a fight]

Carla: What've you done with Ed? Where is my husband, goddammit?

Matt: You say your husband traversed the rift? [Silence] Mrs Strube, what was out there was a spatial rift, a hole in the space-time continuum, a door between two points in space leading to..... somewhere, probably light years away.

Emma: Was?

Carla: Yeah. You said "Was"

Matt: Mrs Strube, I......

Emma: You what?

Matt: I wish there was something I could say...

Carla: About what? ABOUT WHAT?

Matt: We'll be moving our equipment out now. Sorry to have inconvenienced you. I hope you understand, we had to..... to...... measure the phenomenon. We weren't to know.
Carla: KNOW? KNOW WHAT?
[Matt backs out of the door and exits]

Emma: what did he mean?

Carla: EMMA! GO LOOK OUT BACK!
[Emma looks at her, grasps her meaning and rushes out of the room. A few seconds later, she runs back in]

Carla: WELL?

Emma: It's gone, Carla, it's gone.
[They look at each other. Lights fade to black]

Sages was performed by the Zed-Bed Theatre Company
At the White Bear Theatre, 138 Kennington Park Road, London SE11
25th April – 13th May 2000.

Director: Peter Cunningham

Cast:
Gautama - Gunther Wurger
Rinzai - Rob Widdicombe
Bodhidharma - Martin Cooper

Sages

Blackout. There are three dark shapes seated on the floor. Lights come on suddenly to reveal three men seated on the ground, dressed only in white robes. They sit in a rough semi-circle facing the audience. They are Gautama, Bodhidharma and Rinzai. Next to Gautama is a Flower (Red Rose, Lotus blossom, it doesn't really matter) and next to Rinzai is a small pile of stones.

Gautama: It is remarkable how unremarkable things are.

Bodhidharma:Like what?

Rinzai: He means like homogenized.

Gautama: I mean like still.

Rinzai: Still?

Gautama: Like descending to a lower state, until still.

Bodhidharma: But still existing?

Gautama: Still existing, but nothing in it moves.

Rinzai: We're all like that.

Bodhidharma: Eventually we are. Sometime soon.

Gautama: [sanctimoniously] No, now. Pause a moment.

Bodhidharma: But if now.... this.... us..... here, what of that?

Rinzai: Are we different? A nonsense?

Gautama: That's not my point. Everything is quiet. Even noise. Noise is very quiet. Different. The same.

Rinzai: Out here, over there, what they are doing is still?

Gautama: It's still because they sleep in it.

Bodhidharma: Do we sleep in this?

Gautama: No. This is drawn.

Rinzai: Drawn?

Gautama: One example of rushing. The rushing of........ silence.

Rinzai: I'm not silent.

Gautama: Everything is quiet. Even noise.

Rinzai: Make sense.

Gautama: Sense makes.

Bodhidharma: He's riddling.

Rinzai: I know. He thinks we don't know anything.

Gautama: I know you don't think. However, thinking alone is not sufficient.

Bodhidharma: I try other things.

Rinzai: Me too.

Gautama: But you do because you think you should.

Bodhidharma: How else?

Gautama: By drift.

Rinzai: This makes nothing. It's just a game.

Gautama: No players.

Rinzai: You're playing.

Gautama: I'm genuine.

Bodhidharma: What's the game?

Gautama: Noughts and Crosses.

Rinzai: Put a cross.

Gautama: I am with a cross.

Bodhidharma: .. But Noughts and Crosses....

Gautama: Scudding the floor it is. I have to drag it.

Bodhidharma: Where?

Gautama: The square.

Rinzai: Why can't we just........ I mean....... this suits me less, a little less than....... before.

Gautama: We have nothing else to do.

Bodhidharma: Is this a hospital?

Gautama: If it is, what are we?

Bodhidharma: Patients?

Rinzai: Nurses?

Gautama: Cleaners. We tend the flowers.
[Gautama picks up a flower which was lying by his side and holds it aloft. Bodhidharma looks puzzled for a moment, then smiles enigmatically.]

Gautama: You are my inheritor.

Bodhidharma: What inheritance?

Gautama: This flower.

Bodhidharma: It's dead.

Gautama: So is everything else.

Bodhidharma: Not me.

Rinzai: Not me either.

Gautama: If you think about it, you are.

Bodhidharma: I can't be. I just ate. I just made beans on toast. I just walked outside. I just walked over here. I just.....

Gautama: You just about hold together. All your fragments are wholes.

Bodhidharma: That's evolution.

Gautama: It's glue.

Bodhidharma: You say these things. You must be alive.

Gautama: I'm passing time. It's not the same thing.

Bodhidharma: Look at yourself. You're unbalanced. You don't know what you're saying. I had an aunt, in North wales. She made flowers her life. She knew roots, she made..... she put things on people that made them well. Wounds were healed, for Heaven's sake!

Gautama: A wound is another life, a life is another wound.

Rinzai: You're playing with words.

Bodhidharma: Charlatan!

Gautama: You force me to it!

Bodhidharma: I want you to stop.

Gautama:OK, I've stopped. Do you know any good jokes?

Bodhidharma: This man, he sat on the side of a hill all his life.

Gautama: Didn't he shit?

Bodhidharma: He shit.

Gautama: And eat, and sleep?

Bodhidharma: Yes..

Gautama: He sat on the side of a hill all his life?

Bodhidharma: No.

[Gautama laughs hysterically]

Gautama: It's a good joke.

Rinzai: OK. A man sits against a tree, asleep. He dreams he's sitting against a tree asleep. When he wakes up, he doesn't know which man he is.

Gautama: I don't like that.

Rinzai: You laughed at the other one.

Gautama: But not that. It seems too true.

Rinzai: That's why it's funny.

Gautama: That's why it hurts.

Rinzai: You just prefer him.

Gautama: No, I prefer a woman.

Bodhidharma: You're too old.

Gautama: I'm too scared.

Rinzai: I don't think of you as scared.

Gautama: I'd prefer you didn't think of me at all.

Rinzai: Why?

Gautama: Because I don't know which man I am.
[Rinzai studies his palm. Then he picks up a stone and puts it in Gautama's hand.]

Rinzia: Take this.

Gautama: Why?

Rinzai: You'll be the one with the stone.

Bodhidharma: What about me?

Gautama: You're a bag of shit.

Bodhidharma: Oh?

Gautama: You wanted to know.

Bodhidharma: No. Not that I didn't. It isn't anyway true.

Gautama: If it is, you shit yourself.

Rinzai: That's true for everyone.

Gautama: No, not me.

Rinzai: You, yes.

Gautama:No, not me.

Rinzai: Because you're a product.

Gautama: What of?

Rinzai: Of what coagulated in your mother's body....

Gautama: And what then?

Rinzai: And then you had to endure..... this.

Gautama: Because I....

Rinzai: Because you were born. Which is another word for glue.

Gautama: Glue?

Rinzai: Your mother ate burgers and stuff?

Gautama: Of course.

Rinzai: She accumulated you?

Gautama: Well....

Rinzai: So you're those burgers.

Gautama: Too simple.

Rinzai: Not simple enough. The mystery is, why not nothing?

Gautama: That is the mystery. But my mother didn't make me.

Rinzai: Oh yeah, smart arse? So who did?

Gautama: It's not a question of being made. It's just things growing in the appointed place.

Rinzai: Eh? Appointed?

Bodhidharma: I know what he means. Like, you know when I open the fridge and there's some stuff been in there a month and only some of it grows mould. Bread, cheese, not Garlic, not Potato.

Gautama: That's not what I mean. I mean Gravity pulls down. On the way down, things sometimes stick. Bigger things come out of that.

Bodhidharma: Huh. That sounds really scientific. Sure has me convinced. [to Rinzai] You too?

Gatama: That's what it is.

Rinzai: [to Bodhidharma] Are you gonna listen to this?

Gautama: Listen to it. Believe it.

Bodhidharma: Ah.. this New Age shit. Who can hack it?

Gautama: New Age? That ain't me.

Rinzai: So.. the guy in the dream?

Gautama: What about him?

Rinzai: Who was he?

Gautama: I guess he was you.

Rinzai: Me? I'm not in the joke. I just told it.

Gautama: [Sits erect. adopts a stern expression. Speaks loud and pompous] Cut it out.
Now! SHOW ME YOUR ORIGINAL FACES!

Bodhidharma: I AM BODHIDHARMA!

Rinzai: I AM... RINZAI!

Gautama: I AM GAUTAMA!
[Suddenly a distant bell chimes nine times]

Gautama: It's time.

Bodhidharma: Yes. It's time.

Rinzai: We must return to the world to teach the way to others.

Gautama: The sound of one hand clapping.

Bodhidharma: Does a dog have Buddha nature?
[Suddenly a woman in a nurses uniform appears]

Nurse: How are we today, Mr Stephanov?

Gautama: Gautama.

Nurse: Oh. I'm sorry. Could you, and Bodhidharma and Rinzai come back in now, please? It's time for your medication.
[They all get up. stand facing in different directions looking confused and bewildered. Lights fade slowly to black]

See Ya Later was first performed by the Zed-Bed Theatre Company
At the White Bear Theatre, 138 Kennington Park Road, London SE11
25th April – 13th May 2000

Director: Valerie Dent

Cast:
Rose - Saskia Vale
Guy - Gerard Gilroy
Rudolph - Greg Jarvis

See Ya Later

Characters: Guy: A man in his late 30s.
Rose: Guy's wife. A similar age.
Rudolph: A man in his 30s.

[Blackout. Suddenly we hear a loud crash. Two figures lying on a bed are dimly visible. One of them reaches for the bedside lamp. Lights come up]

ROSE: What was that?

GUY: mmmm?

ROSE: Wake up. I heard somethin'

GUY: That's three times.

ROSE: Look, are you gonna check?

GUY: There's the phone. Call the cops. That's what we pay taxes for.

ROSE: Godammit! You are a cop!

GUY: Yeah. An' I'm off duty.

ROSE: Are you gonna let me, your darling wife,risk my life? There could be anyone in the house. I'm a woman for God's sake!

GUY: It's been so long I almost forgot.

ROSE: Don't get smart with me. Are you gonna lie there while some mean sonofabitch prowls the house? He's probably got a gun. He could come in here.

GUY: Great. Maybe he's a marriage guidance counsellor.

ROSE: GUY! [She pushes him out of bed]

GUY: Ok....... I'll go see shall I? That's a good idea. I'm so glad I thought of it. [sarcastically] Hey Rose while I'm up would you like a frothy coffee, or maybe a T-bone with all the trimmings? [She ignores him. He puts on a dressing gown, he walks to the door and opens it. Outside is a small bespectacled man all dressed In black with a balaclava. Rose screams, tries to get up, remains on her feet for a second, then faints]

RUDOLPH: er....hi.

GUY: What do you want?

RUDOLPH: nothing.

GUY: You break in my house at [checks his watch] 3 am......... and you want nothin'?

RUDOLPH: nothin' much. well, er, actually, I wanted some money, if that's ok with you, that is.

GUY: Oh, is that all? that's OK. hey, I'll show you where it is. but, listen, is that all?

RUDOLPH: What d'ya mean? Isn't that enough? That's what burglars usually do isn't it? Take money, I mean.

GUY: Well they do, but I've got a real nice VCR, and you should see our hi-fi, not to mention the TV, dishwasher, my kid's got one of those Playstations. He wouldn't miss it.

RUDOLPH: I don't think I could carry all that. I'll settle for the money. I must say, you're bein' real nice about this. You know, [he laughs] I bought a gun, but if everyone's as nice as you, I might even sell it. God knows, I need the money. I got mouths to feed.

GUY: Wife and Kids?

RUDOLPH: No...... Alligators.

GUY: Alligators?

RUDOLPH: Alligators.

GUY: Are they legal in this state?

RUDOLPH: Nope. But neither is burglary.

GUY: You amaze me.

RUDOLPH: It's true.

GUY: Where'd you get 'em?

RUDOLPH: I picked 'em up in the everglades. They were babies. I took 'em home in a holdall.

GUY: They're a protected species.

RUDOLPH: I feel real guilty about it. But they were so small and lovable, you know?

GUY: And they're not anymore, right?

RUDOLPH: No. I had to buy a new tape measure when Alphonse got to 6 feet. He gets real hungry. Unfortunately, I was out on a heist last week and he ate marmaduke.

[Pause]

RUDOLPH: My cat. Lovely marbled grey colouring. I went into the kitchen and his tail was hanging out of Alphonse's mouth.

GUY: What's the penalty for kidnapping baby alligators?

RUDOLPH: Well, that's the strange thing. It's a five year stretch. Same as for burglary for a first offense. That's how I came up with the idea.

GUY: Couldn't you just take them back?

RUDOLPH: Have you tried taking an 8 ft Alligator on a greyhound bus? They fidget, snap at people. They're nothin' but trouble, man. Sometimes, y'know, I regret the whole thing, I really do.

GUY: How much do you need?

RUDOLPH: Oh..... not that much......say......er....... a thousand spot.

GUY: A grand?

RUDOLPH: You should see how these guys eat. And they're fussy too. It's none of that bully beef in tins for them. You give it to 'em, they just won't touch it. Not good enough for 'em. I really love 'em. They're like, well......... oh, you'll think I'm crazy....

GUY: No, no........ go on.

RUDOLPH: They're my buddies. My only ones actually.

GUY: That's sad. That's real sad.

RUDOLPH: Look, you're a real nice guy.

GUY: Thank you.

RUDOLPH: So I'm not gonna rob you blind. I'm gonna be decent about this. I'll play you for it.

GUY: Play me?

RUDOLPH: You got a deck of cards?

GUY: Yeah. There's some in the bedside drawer. You know, for those sleepless nights.

RUDOLPH: You an insomniac?

GUY: No. My wife likes to talk.

RUDOLPH: The cards.

GUY: Oh yeah. [He goes to the bedside drawer, rummages around and brings out an old, battered pack. Rudolph grabs them and starts dealing] What's it gonna be? Poker? Brag?

RUDOLPH: You know cheat?

GUY: Do I know cheat? Deal, my man.

RUDOLPH: A grand?

GUY: A grand.

RUDOLPH: The rules. I get one past you or you call cheat when it ain't, I win.

GUY: Not the first one out?

RUDOLPH: Listen, I got homes to burgle. I mean, you guys are great, real nice, but I can’t stay all night. Er.... you got anythin’ to drink?

GUY: Tea? Coffee? Water?

RUDOLPH: Not quite what I was thinkin’ of. You got any Tequila?

GUY: Oh. No.
[Rudolph lays down some cards in irritation]

RUDOLPH: Two queens.

GUY: You ever been bitten?

RUDOLPH: Bitten? Lemme show you the scars!

GUY: That’s OK. So they’re not pussycats, huh?

RUDOLPH: These mothers’d eat me for hors d’ouvre. Alphonse opens his mouth, somethin’ organic goes in or he goes apeshit. I mean I told you about Marmaduke. That was one hell of a cat. My closest friend. I told Marmaduke everything.

GUY: So you told him you was plannin’ on Alligators? I mean Marmaduke was up to the minute on that decision?

RUDOLPH: Well, that was a kind of snap decision.

GUY: 2 Aces.

RUDOLPH: Hmmmmm.

GUY: You callin’ me a cheat?

RUDOLPH: er.... yes..... I mean no.

GUY: You can y'know. I could easily be cheatin'.

RUDOLPH: I'll let it pass.
[rose starts to come to]

ROSE: What's...... goin' on?

GUY: Er, hey, Rose, I'd like you to meet er....

RUDOLPH: Call me Rudolph.

GUY: Rudolph. Rose, Rose, Rudolph.

RUDOLPH: Two kings.

GUY: Two kings? [looks at his cards] Two kings?

RUDOLPH: What I said.

GUY: Two......... kings.

RUDOLPH: Fishy ain't it? I could easily be lyin' about that one. But then, there's a grand on it, ain't there?

GUY: I catch you out, I get a grand?

RUDOLPH: For sure. It goes both ways. Didn't I mention that?

GUY: OK..... OK....... I..... think.....you're......... not cheatin'

RUDOLPH: You like art?

GUY: Art? Yeah.

RUDOLPH: I'm lookin' for a painting with Alligators in.

GUY: You are, huh? 3 Twos.

RUDOLPH: Cheat!

GUY: You sure?

RUDOLPH: er..... no. Two nines.

GUY: [peering closely at the cards.] Isn't that three cards?

RUDOLPH: Could be. Could indeed be.
[Rose is now fully awake]

ROSE: What the fuck is goin' on?

GUY: Go back to sleep. One five.

RUDOLPH: One?

GUY: One

ROSE: What is all this?

GUY: What does it look like?

ROSE: He's a crook!

GUY: [to Rudolph] That's what it is. One little old five.

RUDOLPH: hmmm.

GUY: You got a problem?

RUDOLPH: I dunno. Lemme think.

GUY: Why would I cheat on a single card?

RUDOLPH: Given the stakes, it'd be the best time.

GUY: Huh?

RUDOLPH: Look, I miss a cheat, one single cheat, you get a grand. It's taken me hours to get what I got.

ROSE: STOP!

RUDOLPH: Look, it's simple. You're gonna cheat whan I least expect you to. Like now, with a single card.

GUY: Oh. Yeah.

RUDOLPH: Don't play the innocent. You know damn well.

GUY: Maybe I do, maybe I don't.

ROSE: WHAT THE FUCK IS GOIN' ON? I"M CALLIN' THE FUCKIN' COPS

RUDOLPH: [To Guy] You want me to deal with this?

GUY: I'd be grateful.
[She goes over to the phone and starts dialling. She has her back to them. Rudolph pulls out a handkerchief and a bottle. Pours some liquid into the handkerchief. He advances on Rose, clamps the handkerchief over her mouth. There is a brief struggle, then she is still. He lays her on the bed]

RUDOLPH: Handful, ain't she?

GUY: 15 years. I've had this for 15 years. Drives a man nuts in the end.

RUDOLPH: Drove me crazy too. I was married.

GUY: You were? What happened?

RUDOLPH: It was bliss at first. I met this beautiful, and I mean peachy babe through Vital Signs.

GUY: Vital......

RUDOLPH: Signs. Vital Signs. A dating agency.

GUY: Oh.

RUDOLPH: We got on. I took her everywhere with me. Her name was Maria. We was known as JohnandMaria. A single word. An entity. That was us.

GUY: I thought your name was Rudolph.

RUDOLPH: My confirmation name. My mother's choice.

GUY: There was a Saint Rudolph?

RUDOLPH: Obscure isn't it? He's the patron saint of coal.

GUY: Coal?!

RUDOLPH: Yeah, but the role got expanded to include all household heating materials.

GUY: I never heard of him.

RUDOLPH: A much abused saint. You know? There's a nuclear plant in Milwaukee that uses him as a logo.

GUY: How'd you know it's him?

RUDOLPH: He carries a sack of twigs. It's usually twigs, although any combustible material would do. But Plutonium.... well, I draw the line there. I have scruples. Oh shit. This always puts me in mind of Edna.

GUY: Edna.

RUDOLPH: Yeah. My first wife. God rest her eternal soul.

GUY: She's dead?

RUDOLPH: [Swallows hard and looks down] Yeah.

GUY: I....er......I'm.......

RUDOLPH: Don't be. There was nothin' I could do.

GUY: Look.... I don't mean to pry.... I mean you have a perfect right to your privacy but...

RUDOLPH: She was obsessed with technology. She used ta love goin' on factory tours. Visits to refineries, trips to see the production line at General Motors. She saw almost every large industrial complex in the midwest in the ten years we were married. She subscribed to every journal she could lay her hands on. Inflateable Dwelling Research Quarterly, Welding Technology Gazette, Blast Furnace World...... you name it. The house was stacked this high with it all. It makes me weep to think about it.

GUY: What....

RUDOLPH: What happened? You wanna know? You really wanna know?

GUY: Look. I can see this is painful for you.

RUDOLPH: No....no....This has gotta be said. it's an exorcism for me. It's a long time since I.... since I......

GUY: Talked about it.

RUDOLPH: [sobbing] Yeah.
[silence]

RUDOLPH: She..... that is.....we... went on a visit to a steel mill. You know, the molten steel pours out of this huge vat and gets rolled, pressed, extruded into sheets and bars and stuff. It's a fascinating process, believe me. When it's poured, it glows so bright you need goggles just to look at it. We was on a big gantry above the vat. It was spectacular. Sparks of molten metal flying everywhere. She had a particular interest in the extrusion process, you know, how they mould it, squeeze it, draw it out thinner and thinner until....

GUY: You get wire.

RUDOLPH: Yeah. So she wanted to see it all. Start to finish. So we started at the vat. On the gantry. She wanted to see it splash into the runnels and flow down to the rollers. She just had to [sobs] had to see it close up. She couldn't quite see..... so......she.... leaned over the vat to get a better look and..... and......

GUY: I get the picture. Look..... I'm sorry.

RUDOLPH: It's OK. It was a long time ago. But we was twin spirits. The only time. The only one for me. I never loved again.

GUY: What about Maria?

RUDOLPH: It was sex.

GUY: Look to the future.

RUDOLPH: When Edna went, so did everything else. I tried to convince myself that pleasure could take the place of love. I was wrong.

GUY: Listen. A grand? I can do that.

RUDOLPH: We're still playin' ain't we?

GUY: er...

RUDOLPH: So play. I honour my word. What was the call?

GUY: One five.

RUDOLPH: Cheat!

GUY: Er... listen....

RUDOLPH: Cheat!

GUY: [turns the card over] No.
[Silence. Rudolph slumps.]

GUY: I'm sorry. When I was kid, my sister betty an' me played games. Canasta, Checkers, Ludo, Monopoly the works. She always cheated. Always found a way. I decided never to be like that, so I.....I.....

RUDOLPH: Never cheat.

GUY: No.

RUDOLPH: Here's my wallet [pulls it out and hands it to him] you should find a grand in there.

GUY: Thanks, but, well maybe it won't be necessary.

RUDOLPH: What d'ya mean?

GUY: Your Alligators. How much do they eat?

RUDOLPH: At least their own body weight in a week. Alphonse in particular. He's voracious.

GUY: So the weight of, say, a human being wouldn't be a big meal?

RUDOLPH: A human being?

GUY: [looks at the prostrate form of Rose] That's what I was wonderin', yeah.

RUDOLPH: I couldn't, I mean.... it'd be against my ethics. I'm a burglar, yeah, but it's through necessity. Edna had strict moral principles. Kinda rubbed off on me. Believe me, even this is hard. To do this I had to promise myself. So much, no more. Feed the pets. That's all I want. I hate animal cruelty. Either I take people's belongings or starve poor dumb brutes. I mean that's an ethical dilemma, ain't it?

GUY: Two grand.

RUDOLPH: I'll back the trailer up to your porch. help me drag her out.
[they get up and drag her body toward the door. Lights out]

[Lights come up in Rudolph's house. His lounge. Rose is in a chair, her hands tied behind her. She is gagged. Guy and Rudolph are eating buscuits and drinking coffee. Rudolph is reading a newspaper. A gun, a bottle and a handkerchief are on he table.]

GUY: So when can we do it?

RUDOLPH: Need to wait until Alphonse is hungry. He makes a kind of loud snarling noise. Show's he's gettin' feisty. In need of a little cullinary stimulation.

GUY: How long will that be?

RUDOLPH: lemme see.... Alphonse ate at..... 8 pm.......that's about [looks at his watch] 7 hours ago. And that was a sheep. So I'd say...... could be hours.

GUY: Ok. I need to get some sleep. I'm wacked. What do we do about the bones?

RUDOLPH: Not a problem. They'll eat those too.

GUY: They will? Don't they shit any evidence?

RUDOLPH: Not much. Digest almost everything. Very efficient creatures, Alligators. Alphonse learns tricks too.

GUY: Tricks?

RUDOLPH: I'm teaching him to count.

GUY: That's amazing.

RUDOLPH: Ain't it? I got cages of small rodents. He likes live food, y'know. Rats, mice, gerbils, that kinda thing. I've taught him up to 3. I hold three up in a jar and he has to pat the floor three times before he gets 'em.

GUY: You should write a paper about that. Nature magazine would be falling over themselves.

RUDOLPH: It's nothin'.

GUY: No, no, it's a real breakthrough. Before you know it, he'll be reading Kafka.

RUDOLPH: You're making fun.

GUY: I wouldn't do that. Listen, man, I respect you. Perserverance is a virtue. A real virtue.

RUDOLPH: Well, it has taken time.

GUY: For sure! Teaching that fucker must take patience.

RUDOLPH: He ain't a fucker. That's Alphonse you're talkin' about. [Gets up and grabs guy's shirt] You don't call him that! Alright? You don't call him that!

GUY: [backing away, hands up] OK.....OK..... slip of the tongue..... No problem.......no problem.......alright?

[Rose starts to come to. She makes muffled noises behind the gag]

RUDOLPH: Shit!

GUY: Got any more of that stuff?

RUDOLPH: It was Ether. It's over there on the table, but I can't use too much. Might affect Alphonse. He's sensitive like that.

GUY: What about the other one?

RUDOLPH: Matilda's secondary in my affections. Alphonse has this great personality. he's got a real sense of humour. eating marmaduke was his idea of a practical joke. it backfired, but hey, I could see by his grin that he meant well.

GUY: Don't Alligators always grin? I mean, it's a bone structure thing, isn't it?

RUDOLPH: I can tell when Alphonse is amused. Like when we play Fetch the Pigeon.

GUY: Fetch the Pigeon?

RUDOLPH: I catch pigeons, truss them up and throw them for Alphonse.

GUY: My God, that's cruel.

RUDOLPH: Yeah. I oughtta jus' give him the food. I know it tantalises him, but, hey, he has to pay for his keep. Gimme somethin' in return, y'know?

GUY: I meant the pigeons.

RUDOLPH: Aaaaah! They're vermin. What the hell? I was doin' a public service. I know a guy. Rochester, number 128 down the street. He catches pigeons and electrocutes them. He has a generator in his yard, 10,000 volts, right up the beak. watches them turn black. compared to that, this is actually quite humane.

GUY: Listen, you mind if I grab some sleep?

RUDOLPH: Go right ahead. There's the couch.
[Guy goes over to the couch, lies down and closes his eyes]

RUDOLPH: [To Rose] I guess you feel pretty bad about this, but well, look at it this way. It's for the greater good. Look, you comfortable? don't worry, I'll put you out when Alphonse gets peckish. It'll be painless. [Muffled noises from behind the gag] Nothin' ta worry about. Like a visit to the dentist...... All the same.......I'm sorry it has to be this way...... [More muffled noises] [Silence]

RUDOLPH: My Grandfather was abducted by aliens. Did you know that? [She shakes her head] I guess not. Late one night in July 1956 he was sleepin' in a hotel in Nantucket. Business trip. Had a few drinks, yeah, but not inebriated. if you know what I mean. Suddenly this ghostly shaft of green light beams into the room. Straight through the window. Cut through the dust. Next thing he knows, he's in a saucer out in space. This was reported in the papers. He remembers lookin' out this porthole an' seein' the Earth. I know, I know, it doesn't sound plausible, does it? That isn't all. They dissected him. They used rays to do it. And you know what else? They drained all his blood and then put it back again. Through all that, they kept him alive somehow. Guess they're more advanced than us, huh? The police found him lying in the road near Fairfield, Connecticut. no body hair left, naked. Now how'd you account for that?
[She shakes her head]

RUDOLPH: And he lived to be 93. Died in the fall of 1989. Lived to see the Berlin Wall come down. I was in the geriatric wing of Fairfield County Hospital when it was on TV. All he could say was "That's them. They're comin' back.". Sure spooked me. That was the last thing I ever heard him say. I left that afternoon, and I never saw him again. When he was young, he worked in teachests. This was before the plastics revolution. In those days it was a trade. You could get certificates. Gave it up though. One time he took forty winks in one and they nailed it up and shipped his ass to Wyoming.
[Silence]

RUDOLPH: Listen, baby, you mind if I go check on Alphonse? He's been too quiet.

[He exits. She starts to struggle frantically to escape her bonds. As she does so, the some really frenetic music (like 'flight of the bumblebee' for example) plays. Just as the music comes to an end, she frees herself, rips off the gag and picks up the gun. She turns around just in time to see Rudolph return. She points the gun at him. He puts his hands up. Blackout]

[Lights up on Rudolph's living room. Rudolph and Guy are sitting on chairs, trussed up. Rudolph is gagged. Rose is sitting on the sofa, drinking a can of beer and reading a magazine.]

GUY: Rose, darling, I'm thirsty.

ROSE: You are? Would you like some beer?

GUY: Yeah.

ROSE: Say please.

GUY: Please.

ROSE: Say 'Yes please, Rose'.

GUY: Rose...... look......

ROSE: You want beer or don't ya?

GUY: Yes please, Rose.

[She goes over and holds the can under his nose then takes it away again]

ROSE: Ask me later, if you're still thirsty.

GUY: Rose?
[She ignores him]

GUY: Rose, look, I realise you're probably a bit pissed off right now, but, well, I'm sorry. I mean, I wouldn't have gone through with it. Just before I went to sleep I was thinkin', well, I think we scared her enough. When I wake up, I'll untie her and take her home.

ROSE: What about the money?

GUY: The money.

ROSE: You were payin' him for his services, I trust? Murder bein' a capital offense.

GUY: I...... we.......

ROSE: Don't bother makin' up a lie, I found it in your jeans.

GUY: You went through my pockets? That ain't fair, Rose, you hear me? That's deceit, that's what that is.
[silence]

GUY: Look, Rose, OK, OK, I've learnt my lesson. I'll try harder at our relationship. I'll even go see Dr. Goodhew. OK? Rose?
[Silence]

GUY: Rose? What're you waitin' for, Rose?

ROSE: What am I waiting for? What am I waiting for, Guy?
[She puts the gag on him. There's the loud sound of hungry Alligators snarling]

ROSE: Alphonse and Matilda, that you?.

[Lots of muffled noises from the gagged men as lights slowly fade to black]

Stale Cabbage was first performed by Fresh Productions
At the White Bear Theatre, 138 Kennington Park Road, London SE11
12th – 17th July 2005.

Director: Maria Griffin

Cast:
Cutter - Enid Gayle
Quill - Elaine Smitthers
Nurse - Dominic James

The play was originally written for two men (Cutter and Quill) and a female nurse. For this production, the play was given a few 'tweaks' and the gender roles were reversed to two women and a male nurse.

Stale Cabbage

[Lights up on two old men sitting in wheelchairs. There's a small round coffee table to their right with magazines on, and two cups.]

Quill: You shouldn't have touched.

Cutter: She didn't mind. I think she liked it. Appreciated the attention. You should listen to me. I know a thing or two about women.

Quill: Pah! Show me the bruises.

Cutter: She was in my room. I saw the way she looked at me. It was the glad eye. Definitely the come-hither.

Quill: You can't possibly believe she saw anything in you. You shouldn't have done it.

Cutter: It was only a little touch. A little exploration under the uniform. She's lonely, you know.

Quill: What was she doing in your room?

Cutter: Emptying my bed pan.

Quill: I can see now how she might have been overcome with desire.

Cutter: She was flattered.

Quill: She was repelled. I am disgusted. Look at you. She wanted that? I think not.

Cutter: You're jealous.

Quill: Jealous? I feel nothing but pity. To be so pathetic. And to let her see that. Where's your pride? At least I'm slim. She could go for me. But you.....

Cutter: I think she likes me.

Quill: She did. Before that happened. she thought you refined. Intelligent. Of course, I knew the truth. Bluster was all it was.

Cutter: At least I can summon some bluster. Look at you. I can already see your tombstone. It'll say "He waited for something to happen". Nothing comes to he who waits. You should know that by now. You should have tried something else. Something risky, brave, but you preferred to wait. THAT is pathetic.

Quill: I have retained at least the vestiges of decorum. I know how to behave around a woman. I gave her Chrysanthemums. Did I tell you that? That counts. That most definitely counts.

Cutter: Don't lie to yourself. Your life is slipping away. Don't you think she knows that? She needs someone protective..... viable...... potent. If it came to it.... she'd prefer me. And at teatime? Who'd you think she'll feed first? She'll have thought it over by then. She'll recognise I still have spirit.

Quill: She'll recognise an imbecile. That's what she'll recognise. An imbecile with one foot in the grave and the other on a banana skin. She knows you'll be gone soon.

Cutter: I think otherwise.

Quill: You've got a nasty cough. I haven't heard that before.

Cutter: Just a cough. It’s not important.

Quill: That’s how it starts.

Cutter: If it was important, I’d know.

Quill: That’s how it always starts.

Cutter: What’s the time?

Quill: Time, time. What does it matter what time it is?

Cutter: It matters to me. There’s always another second that won’t be mine again.

Quill: You could make up a time. It’d be as true as any other.

Cutter:[Musing] Passing the time.

Quill: What?

Cutter: We’re passing the time. Only really it’s passing us.

Quill: How long have we been here?

Cutter: I don’t know. Ten, twenty.... It seems a long time.

Quill: I remember the thunderstorm last week.

Cutter: Was it last week?

Quill: Or the week before.

Cutter: That’s it, isn’t it.

Quill: What’s it?

Cutter: That's the point. Time. Time is memory. They're the same thing. The worse your memory, the shorter your time. And vice versa.

Quill: Say again?

Cutter: Vice versa. The shorter your time, the fewer your memory.

Quill: But there are more memories. More things gone.

Cutter: But they slip away to escape you. Like a crowd crushing through a thin doorway. Trying to get away.

Quill: Away from what?

Cutter: From the dark, the dark.

Quill: But they run into the dark.

Cutter: Yes, ironic. The short time between knowing and forgetting. The shorter your time.....

Quill: It's not always like that.

Cutter: But usually.

Quill: Usually. I'll concede.

Cutter: I was standing outside a tall building.

Quill: Eh?

Cutter: I remember something. Something I did. Somewhere I was.

Quill: What of it?

Cutter: Outside this building. It was grey.

Quill: Buildings are usually grey.

Cutter: And I couldn't get in.

Quill: I wonder why? Why always grey?

Cutter: I needed to know who I was going to see.

Quill: It must be cheaper.

Cutter: I knew they wouldn't let me in if I couldn't tell them who I'd come to see.

Quill: Or maybe it's a conspiracy. Someone at some time or other, by some power invested, once decided to enforce grey as a rule. A kind of law. By people who don't like other people to be happier than they are. Grey is a leveller. That's it. Everything the same. No qualities, superficial or otherwise. Nothing can be beautiful. Then everything must be. Just be. Being without qualities.

Cutter: I could imagine myself standing in front of the reception desk. It would have been a black desk. Tall, with a buzz-button on it. Not so much a desk, as a barrier. The Boulder Dam, for the flood of insults [he chuckles]. A young woman would hear my buzzing and come out, holding a cheese sandwich.

Quill: They wouldn't do that. It's not professional. Not the image they'd want to project.

Cutter: Or something. A typewriter.

Quill: Too heavy. She wouldn't take it with her. Not just to see who's there.

Cutter: What does it matter? [Cutter start coughing loudly]

Quill: It obviously matters to you. Or you wouldn't have mentioned it.

Cutter: It was only a little aside.

Quill: Every single thing a person says is important. It tells you what they chose not to say.

Cutter: So I knew I wouldn't be able to tell her anything.

Quill: Why would you need to?

Cutter: To get in. To meet the man I'd come to see.

Quill: Who?

Cutter: I've told you. I couldn't remember.

Quill: Not up to much, are you?

Cutter: So I stood outside. On the pavement. And it suddenly dawned on me.

Quill: What? Who you'd come to see?

Cutter: No! I told you, I couldn't remember his name.

Quill: You knew it was a he. Rather than a she?

Cutter: I think so. Yes...... I'm certain of it.

Quill: You think so? Some things it's better to be sure about.

Cutter: I said I was certain.

Quill: There was a hesitation. Momentary, but there. Very much there.

Cutter: And it dawned on me....

Quill: You said that.

Cutter: dawned on me that if I didn't know who I wanted to see, well, I had no business being there. Am I right or not?

Quill: Recap.

Cutter: Me. Tall grey building among others. Me, outside. Man I want to see, inside. I know who I am. I don't know who he is. Don't know what I want, although it could have been insurance. It could have been....... it........ and so....... and so....... therefore..... the corollary....... I can't get in.

Quill: When did this happen?

Cutter: I don't know. I remember it, but not when.

Quill: You're without hope.

Cutter: So are you. I've seen you clutching things.

Quill: What things?

Cutter: Your Bible. You don't just pick it up anymore. You clutch it. Like a crucifix. Like a gun. It used to be on the top shelf. Now..... now, it's by the bed. I see. I notice.

Quill: I can still stand. It's purely accidental that it's where I can reach it.

Cutter: At night? It's always at night when you reach for it. I see. I notice.

Quill: Go on with your story.

Cutter: It was then I remembered my briefcase. It had a card with his name on it.

Quill: Whose name?

Cutter: The man I want to see.

Quill: Do you still want to see him?

Cutter: I looked down at my hand, and no briefcase. I'd left it in the room I'd just come from.

Quill: What room?

Cutter: It was brown.

Quill: What's the significance of the colour?

Cutter: I don't know. It was just brown. It's not important. What's important was......

Quill: Everything. Every colour people choose is important. It tells you what colours they didn't choose.

Cutter: All of them? It could have been any other colour. That tells you nothing.

Quill: Oh, but it does.Within the context of a room, your choice would be limited.

Cutter: No it wouldn't.

Quill: Yes it would. You wouldn't have a black bathroom. No-one would.

Cutter: That's nonsense. I've been in black rooms.

Quill: Not bathrooms.

Cutter: But rooms. Rooms!

Quill: When? When have you been in a black room?

Cutter: Dorothy had a black room.

Quill: Did you know Dorothy?

Cutter: Dorothy Fenwick?

Quill: Dorothy.... Dorothy.... I can't remember her second name. Could have been Fenwick. And she did not.

Cutter: Did not?

Quill: Have a black room.

Cutter: I stood in it once. I remember. And I sat down too. She had red chairs. Velvet. There was a little table with brass corners and a glass top. Chocolate biscuits. McVitie's. A teapot. Blue. Two cups. Pink. She was sitting in the other red velvet chair smiling at me. We talked about weapons.

Quill: Weapons? Who talks about weapons?

Cutter: She was heavily politicised.

Quill: Not what springs to mind.

Cutter: Oh. And what does spring to mind?

Quill: Not the Dorothy I knew. Must be another.

Cutter: She had a polkadot dress on.

Quill: Don’t see much of those these days.

Cutter: Marks and Sparks, it was.

Quill: Eh?

Cutter: You know. The shop.

Quill: Yes, yes, I know. I wasn’t born yesterday.

Cutter: I saw the label.

Quill: She was facing you. How could you see?

Cutter: Before we went into the room. When she let me in. In the hallway. She was smiling then, too. And we went into the room.

Quill: Is this the brown room or the black one.

Cutter: Neither. It was blue.

Quill: You said black.

Cutter: It was blue.

Quill: And what about the brown room?

Cutter: Which one?

Quill: The one you came from to see the man in the grey building. Who was in that room?

Cutter: I was.

Quill: Apart fom you.

Cutter: I don't know.

Quill: It's important. I always make a point of knowing who I'm in a room with. It's only common sense. And good manners.

Cutter: Why?

Quill: If you don't know who they are, you can't address them properly.

Cutter: That's ridiculous. If I didn't know who they were, I wouldn't want to address them.

Quill: You wanted to address the man in the grey building. You didn't know who he was.

Cutter: You're nitpicking. His name was on a card. In my briefcase. I'd just left it behind, that's all.

Quill: In the brown room.

Cutter: All you do is pick holes. You're beginning to get on my nerves.

Quill: You never said that before. swine!

Cutter: It's called being polite.

Quill: It's deception. that's what it is.

Cutter: Are you sure I never told you?

Quill: I'd remember a thing like that.

Cutter: Our time is short. So is our memory. I shouldn't have said that, forgive me.

Quill: Never go to sleep on an argument. My mother always said that.

Cutter: You forgive me?

Quill: How long have we been here?

Cutter: Do you forgive me?

Quill: How long?

Cutter: It seems a long time. I don't remember anymore.

[Ther's a long pause. They fall silent. Quill pulls at his earlobe and grimaces.]

Cutter: Listen!

Quill: What is it?

Cutter: I hear crockery. I smell stale cabbage. It's teatime. [Quill can barely control his glee] I'll be first, you see. Pay attention and you'll see how she looks. How she smiles with her eyes.

[At this moment, a nurse enters carrying a tray]

Cutter: Evening Nurse Midlin. Have you got a little something for me?

[She crosses and places the tray on Quill's lap.]

Nurse: Here you are sweetheart.

Cutter: What about me?

Nurse: Well, Mr Cutter. Here's how it is. You get your food when I get a little something from you.

Cutter: Ooh.

Nurse: An apology, sweetheart, An apology. Then in a few months I might be prepared, given that you can behave in a civilised manner, to treat you like an adult again.

[She exits. Quill is devouring his food ravenously his face radiant with triumph. Cutter looks at him.]

Cutter: Did you hear that? Sweetheart! She called me sweetheart!

[Cutter stares straight ahead. Quill continues to eat. The lights fade to blackout.]

Start was first performed by the Fourth Wall Theatre Company
At the White Bear Theatre, 138 Kennington Park Road, London SE11
3rd – 14th November 1998.

Director: Sona Vyas

Cast:
Annie - Tracey Selfe
Petula - Grenita Vitte
Rod - Mark Hodges

Start.

An apartment. Petula and Annie are having a conversation.

Petula: Last night, I had an idea.

Annie: Sometimes I feel like true, permanent happiness is just a hog's grunt away.

Petula: I ate an artichoke last night. My first time. Jose' took me to La Belle Epoch and we smiled at each other, exchanged love tokens, ate artichoke and drank, drank, drank Claret and Coriander Supernova.

Annie: Coriander....

Petula: Supernova. Two parts Vodka, One part Grenadine, One part Tequila, one part Grand Marnier and.... Coriander juice.

Annie: Coriander juice?

Petula: They put the Coriander in the blender and, hey, you get the juice.

Annie: Sounds disgusting.

Petula: Gets you there. If Pimm's is a bar-room stool, this stuff is the Lincoln Memorial.

Annie: What if Pimm's is a dead skunk floating in a cesspit?

Petula: Jose' was real sweet. He gave me Ivy.

Annie: Ivy?

Petula: A bunch of green Ivy.

Annie: How romantic. What'd he give you on your birthday? A kilo of cement?

Petula: He's inventive. I like that.

Annie: He's either nuts or the last remnant of the Surrealist movement. But he'd need to be about 87 for that, so I guess he's nuts.

Petula: It was when he started kissing my elbow that it started to form, my idea I mean. It was kinda dim at first, like watchin' TV through frosted glass.

Annie: He was kissing your elbow? In a public place? In full view?

Petula: That's not all he did. Next came the real erotic stuff.

Annie: I don't wanna hear it. He should be charged with outraging moral decency.

Petula: I wasn't outraged. In fact, lucky I was sittin' down, 'cos my knees woulda buckled under my weight.

Annie: I can see it all now. Him, stuck to you like a vacuum cleaner on suck, and you sittin' there, with a grin like a suspension bridge.

Petula: You look a little green. Listen, find yourself a Latino. The only thing you have to fear is love overdose. It's a killer, lemme tell ya.

Annie: What was he doin' under the table while he was kissing your elbow? Did he use a monkey wrench? Oh. Silly me, too intellectual. Maybe it was just a monkey.

Petula: And then it came to me.

Annie: The bill?

Petula: How I could make a million bucks and achieve fame and fortune to boot.

Annie: Listen, I'd love to stay, but Mel Gibson's comin' round at eight. We're gonna brush our teeth together.

Petula: It was a flash of insight. All of a sudden I could smell the interior of a Ferrari. The leather. The wood.

Annie: So.... you gonna tell me?

Petula: And have you steal my idea?

Annie: Petula. We've been friends for fifteen years. Would I put anything over on you?

Petula: Can't be too careful. The world's full of wolves.

Annie: Petula.

Petula: Annie.

Annie: Petula........ I .... Don't you trust me?

Petula: All it needs is some venture capital. I already drafted the letter. Tomorrow morning it'll be winging over to a hundred Wall Street high flyers.

Annie: [Sarcastically] Oh shucks Petula..... you just gotta tell me. In an hour I'll be a blackened crisp. Just all burnt up by curiosity.

Petula: Jose's coming round. He'll be here any minute. I'm gonna sloosh down and get slinky. Answer the door if it rings.

Annie: Petula..... [Petula exits] [Resignedly] I can't stay too long. I need to catalogue my stamp collection.
[Annie gets up. She walks over to the door that Petula walked out of.]

Annie: [Quietly] Petula? [No answer]
[Annie sits back down. She picks up her glass, holds it up to the light. She takes a swig.]
[The doorbell rings. Annie looks at the door]

Annie: Well, she said answer it. [She goes over to the door] Who's that? [A muffled voice replies, but is unintelligible] Who? [Another muffled sound. Pause. She opens the door. Rod Askew, a salesman, is there.]

Rod: Hi, my name's Rod.Rod Askew. I represent Multibank Incorporated. I'm here to give you the opportunity of a lifetime.

Annie: Of a lifetime?
[He pushes past her, sits down on the sofa and opens his briefcase]

Rod: Yeah. Ask me a question. Ask me "Do you have any savings plans?".
Annie: Do you know what time it is?

Rod: Do I have savings plans? Do I have one for you? This is tailoring with a big "T". You want a good plan? Pay when you want? Maximum returns for a realistic price? I'm your man, lemme tell ya, flexibility's my middle name.

Annie: Rod Flexibility Askew?

Rod: That's the name that brought me fame! Now, how can I help you?

Annie: Find me a cute, slicked-back Latino. He has to speak English, though. I like Hispanics, don't get me wrong, but I have this irrational desire to converse. I remember at school, this real nice boy, Juan. He had these big eyes? He gazed. If gazing was an Olympic event, he'd get the gold. He gazed. Nobody ever gazed at me that way since. My life ended in the schoolyard.

Rod: Er..... we have this real nice fifteen year plan. It's a retirement top-up. I mean, not that in fifteen years you'll be old enough for.......that is...... It's also neat if you'll wanna move to Florida and get a beachside apartment. That kinda thing. What I meant was.... well..... in fifteen years you'll be...... you'll be..... what will you be?

Annie: He had these beautiful curls hanging over his brow. This kinda sand coloured skin. Well, more like Gold. And he was gentle. All he ever did was look. We never spoke. I used to pray every night that he'd like, come over and whisper some beautiful Spanish nothings in my ear. I mean, even if he said "My carburettor's blocked, you know a good mechanic?", well, if it was Spanish, I wouldn't know the difference, you know what I mean? Of course, I realise that's an absurd example. I mean, at fifteen, he wouldn't have a car, let alone a carburettor. The point, the real point is I was in love. Petula keeps on about Latinos like she discovered a new species. "Latinus Petulicus" [She laughs]. I don't need love overdose. I could see it in his eyes. At fifteen, I was already more experienced in desire than Methuslah's grandmother.

Rod: It has some outstanding advantages....

Annie: It sure does [She closes her eyes.]

Rod: The plan. Starts low and builds. Low startup costs, flexible payments. Listen, let me do your financial profile. [He pulls out a folder] Now. Outgoings. Let's start there. You have any credit debts?

Annie: I used dating agencies for a while. In my twenties. It was one geek after another. I once had this blind date at Happy Hamburger. I shoulda guessed when he suggested it. Any guy that wants to meet at Happy Hamburger has to be threadbare and have a taste bud deficiency. But..... you know what?

Rod: What?

Annie: I went. I was so desperate, I actually went. I sat in Happy Hamburger for two hours. I ate a Big Cheese, three plates of fries, a Rum Baba and a Banana Flood. He stood me up. It was the lowest point of my life. I moved from desperation to desolation. What was it? The sound of my voice? Petula's always meeting guys, Neanderthal passion-bombs that drool for a couple of hours and then explode in her apartment. She's always painting me pictures of her latest erotic fantasia. You know? This must be the afterlife. And I failed the test. You know what Hell is? I'l tell you what Hell is. Hell is having your best friend push her Heaven in your face like it was a grapefruit.

Rod: You're.... not really interested in personal finance, are you?

Annie: Am I ugly? Do you think I resemble Bela Lugosi? Dracula? Peter Cushing?

Rod: Well, no.... you look OK to me.

Annie: You're being polite.

Rod: No, no, I'm not. You look fine. A touch more mascara maybe. Your foundation looks a little flaky, but no, no....... fine. I'd say fine.

Annie: Flaky?

Rod: It's not a big problem. Just a question of applying it right. Listen, my sister Penny runs an image consultancy. She charges the Moon and Stars, but, well, I pick things up real quick. Lemme give you some free advice..

Annie: Really? You'd do that for me?

Rod: Sure. A smile costs nothing. Look. go easy on the eyeshadow. It has to look like a sexy wink, not a subway tunnel. When you apply lipstick, it doesn't need to be like a paint job on your Buick.

Annie: Anything else? Maybe I should get rid of my wooden leg! [She starts to sob]

Rod: Hey! [He offers her his handkerchief] I was only trying to help.
Annie: Why don't you go help Saddam Hussein?

Rod: Look.... er ..... maybe this is the wrong time.
Annie: Maybe it is.

Rod: Well..... I'll just......

Annie: There's the way out [She points]
[Rod gets up and starts collecting his papers]

Rod: OK. I'd better go. [He looks at her intently] Hey. You have nice hands.
Annie: I do?

Rod: Yeah. Best hands I seen since Rosalind.

Annie: Rosalind?

Rod: My ex. That was what I saw first. She was a waitress at Mu Shin over on Michigan Street. I was waiting, I remember it real well, I was waiting for Shark's Fin Soup. The lights were all blue and they were playing Led Zeppelin. "Killing Floor" As I remember.

Annie: How seductive.

Rod: And into this pool of light I was sitting in came these hands holding my soup. And it's not usually the hands I see first. I usually zone into the face, ass, then maybe the legs, feet. Never the hands.

Annie: Thanks for sharin' that with me.

Rod: But this time it was different.

Annie: So, she had good hands, huh?.

Rod: They were resplendent. Like baby corn on the cobs with cherries at the end.
Annie: Sounds like a mutant.

Rod: They were beautiful. I knew I had to know those hands.

Annie: Limited conversation prospects.

Rod: What they did, the hair they combed, the doors they opened, the cigarettes they lit.

Annie: The faces they slapped.

Rod: [Closes his eyes] I could see them joined in prayer. It was a holy experience. Sacred. Transcendent.

Annie: How was the Shark's Fin Soup?

Rod: So-so. Well, dishwater would've been better.
Annie: But it wasn't on the menu? Life's a bitch, ain't it?

Rod: You're laughing at me.
[Silence]

Rod: You are. You think I'm pathetic. An object of ridicule.

Annie: Don't be silly. You just came in here to sell insurance.

Rod: Savings plans, please. I have some self respect.

Annie: I do not laugh at people. I don't have a malicious bone in my body.

Rod: Yeah? Plenty of malicious flesh though, huh?

Annie: That's not fair, I'm a true romantic. I want...... I want.....

Rod: What do you want? I'll tell you what you want.

Annie: And what's that, Sigmund Freud?

Rod: You want our GoldSaver ten year bonus plan. It's got realistic....

Annie: Oh puh-lease.

Rod: It was worth a try.

Annie: You're pushy, ain't you?

Rod: Comes with the job.

Annie: Well. I'm not receptive to your banter. You came, you saw, you screwed up.

Rod: You know? I could get to like you.

Annie: You already blew it.

Rod: I didn't mean to offend.

Annie: No, you haven't. The time's not right, that's all.

Rod: So, you like the Latins?

Annie: It's a new thing for me.

Rod: You just met one?

Annie: No.... Petula....she has.

Rod: Petula?

Annie:: Petula: She's in the bath.

Rod: This isn't your place?

Annie: I live in Selmer Street, two blocks down.

Rod: Oh. Is that nice?

Annie: It's great for insomniacs, drug dealers and sex fiends.

Rod: Sounds.... er ...... instructive.

Annie: Instructive? Yeah, if you wanna learn about the foul side of human nature. If you wanna see pimps beating up their female property, guys jacking up in doorways, and gangs havin' knife fights. I suppose you could see that as instructive. That'd be a good word.

Rod: I gotta go.

Annie: You live.... where?

Rod: Uptown. Apartment block. Entryphone. Closed circuit TV.

Annie: Jacuzzi?

Rod: Well.... yeah..... but communal.

Annie: Tennis court?

Rod: Communal.

Annie: But you're just the same as me.

Rod: I'm sorry?

Annie: No better educated, no better brought up. Why is it you have what I don't?

Rod: I try harder, I guess.

Annie: You couldn't. You couldn't in a thousand years try harder. My dad faded out when I was five. My mother worked herself to an early grave, which, incidentally, I visit each Saturday. She put me through college, kept me from becoming depraved or losing my faith in humanity. She worked, worked, worked..... and then she died.

Rod: Bad stroke.

Annie: Bad stroke? BAD STROKE? You wanna know what I wanted? You hear this and compare it with what I got. When I was workin' as a manicurist at Rupert's Beauty Bar, I used to dream. I used to dream this story for myself. I'd be walking to the subway one night, fingers numb from weilding clippers, and some nice guy in an Armani suit and Raybans would suddenly spot me across the street. He'd rush out, not a care for his own safety, leap over old ladies and mothers with prams, walk on the roofs of taxi cabs and rush after me, protesting his instant, but undying love. I'd ignore him, of course, I don't wanna look too easy. But after a half dozen rash, breathless declarations on one knee, I'd say "Well, OK...... maybe I could do with a drink.". He'd say "Drink? drink? Forget the smalltalk, baby, my private jet's waiting for us at La Guardia, I got champagne on ice, and hey, this is for you". It's then that he pulls out a 5 carat diamond ring, puts it on my pinky and pulls me toward his six-door limousine. I get in and there's a huge bed. He yells "GET GOING" to the chauffeur and pushes a button. Up goes a dark glass screen and he reaches toward me, strokes my cheek gently and...... and.....

Rod: You got a bathroom? I need a piss.

Annie: Yeah, we got one. Petula's in it adorning herself.

Rod: You envy her, doncha?

Annie: Me? Why would I? My real ambition is to be a Carmelite Nun. The spiritual life really draws me, you know? All I wanna do is dig potatoes, spend my days in silent prayer and go to bed, alone, at 7:30.

Rod: Listen, I'm sorry, I'm intruding on your pitiful insecurities.

Annie: That's OK. My best friend does that to me every day.

Rod: Hell bent on Latinos, huh?

Annie: Hell bent.

Rod: With money, though?

Annie: A rich Latino, with a Porsche and a Rolex.

Rod: He'd be a drug dealer.

Annie: I'd turn a blind eye. I don't wanna know how he makes his money. I jus' wanna hang on his arm.

Rod: And ride in his limo.

Annie: Now we understand each other.

Rod: You'd be wasted. I mean, I only met you minutes ago, but I'd say you have integrity.

Annie: It's for sale.

Rod: Come on, take a look at yourself. You want a life? Get out there and live it. All you gotta do is start. Listen, if you don't mind me saying, I..... er ..... find you quite appealing, attractive even.

Annie: You do?

Rod: In an undernourished kinda way, er.... yeah.

Annie: Undernourished? Yeah, well, I've been on a strict diet for five months. The Grape, Cauliflower and Melon diet. I oughtta be a beanpole by now. I've suffered. How would you feel if you went out for a meal with your friends and watched them eat Peking Duck while you tuck into boiled Cauliflower followed by a grape?

Rod: Lousy.

Annie: And people think you're a freak. Anorexic. Ready to hear voices from God and murder the Pope. It doesn't enhance your social life. And now, Petula's the only friend I have. And that's only because she likes to have someone truly pathetic she can gloat over.

Rod: You gotta snap outta this. Look. Why don't you and me go downtown? Have a slap-up meal? Clam Chowder, Seafood Grill followed by Brandy Snaps and Coffee? What d'ya say?

Annie: With you?

Rod: Yeah. Me. Anything wrong with that?

Annie: Look. Don't take offense, but....

Rod: No?
Annie: I'm sorry. I'm too vulnerable right now.

Rod: It was insensitive of me to ask.

Annie: No..... no..... I was flattered. Any other time......

Rod: Yeah. Maybe some other time.

Annie: Yeah. Some other.

Rod: I really got to go. [He picks up his case, jacket and starts for the door] Here's my card. You change your mind, call me.

Annie: Yep.

Rod: Well, 'bye.

Annie: See ya.
[Rod exits. Annie gets up and looks in the mirror]

Annie: Undernourished? Maybe a few more grapes.

[Petula re-enters, in a glamorous red dress.]
Petula: Who was that at the door?

Annie: A salesman. I sent him packing.

Petula: Listen, Annie, I gotta go. Jose' phoned my mobile. I'm meeting him at Roderigo's at eight. Lobster Thermidor here I come.

Annie: Have a great time.

Petula: What about you?

Annie: Oh. I'll finish this [she holds up her glass] and let myself out. My stamp collection.....

Petula: Needs cataloguing, yeah. Look. Things'll get better for you. I'm sure they will. Things will...... will.....

Annie: Get better. [She smiles]

Petula: That's the spirit.

Annie: All I have to do is start.

Petula: Listen, I'm behind time. take care.
[Petula exits]
[Annie sips her glass of wine, stares morbidly at the table. She spots Rod's card, which is still there. She picks it up and looks at it].

Annie: All I have to do is start.......
[Lights fade to blackout]

Up The Hill was first performed by the Twice As Loud Theatre company at:
the Landor Theatre, Clapham, London SW9
20th November – 6th December 1997

Cast:

Maureen –	Anne Corcoran
Pat –	Maurice McParland
Michael –	Ivan Dalmedo
Stage Manager	Paul Crook
Lighting	Sarah Doonican
Sound	Patrick Dixon
	Rob Widdicombe

Up The Hill

[Maureen and her Fiance Pat are sitting in a Dublin public house.]

Maureen: When I was a child, I wasn't a good girl. My mother caught me in the cellar with Billy O'Hara. He was showing me his worm. Mother tore into us like a hawk and says it wasn't a proper thing for a girl my age. Billy went home with a cauliflower ear. I was sent up. I sat up there and pulled the eyes out of teddy. I got whacked for that. And Ted, blind forever, was forever my accuser. I kept the buttons on the shelf and after a while, a few weeks it was, they stopped being eyes. He never saw anything I did after that.

Pat: It was only a toy.

Maureen: It was a part of my living soul. Those eyes always reflected me. Late at night I looked at them. They always brought back my sins. I swore then that I would never look underneath a man, inside his clothes I mean, until....

Pat: Holy Mary! Don't be so bloody serious all the time. It was a long time ago.

Maureen: I carry my cross.

Pat: Your Mam's long gone.Pushing up daisies. Can't you let it go? You've me now.

Maureen: Now it hurts me more. She's not here to argue. If I go my ways now, I'll only blame myself.

Pat: Jesus! You need a bloody shrink, you do.

Maureen: I'm away home now. Take me?

Pat: Are you not comin' up the hill then?

Maureen: Home. Now. I'll go mesel' if not with you.

Pat: For fuck's sake.

Maureen: Stop that Pat. It mars you.

Pat: What does?

Maureen: Profanity. I've noticed it from you more now you're at that warehouse.

Pat: It's nothin'. Just the men. It's what they say down there.

Maureen: Well. Keep it in. It's not well liked.

Pat: Come up, Maur. It's nice on the brow. The wind'll blow the sweat off ya.

Maureen: Do think she has any influence?

Pat: Who?

Maureen: The Virgin.

Pat: [Shrugs] Search me.

Maureen: I always pray to Her. Never to Him. I should, I know, but I feel like I understand Her. And her, me.

Pat: You're both women. That'll be it.

Maureen: It's more than that. She's all women. My home's there. With Her.

Pat: I'm gettin' another. G and T?

Maureen: I have to....

Pat: Just one, for God's sake. One more. Then go.

Maureen: OK. One more. One, mind. [pause] Then go.

[Pat gets up and exits to go to the bar. Maureen starts to talk to herself]

Maureen: He doesn't see. It'll be so much fairer when we're gone. No bodies. No more men and their muscles. Us and our babies. We'll all be the same.

[Pat returns]

Pat: G and T.

Maureen: What's that?

Pat: Vodka. I felt like one.

[They sit in silence, sipping at their drinks. Michael O'Finnessy enters, walks over to their table and sits without being asked]

Michael: Hello everybody.

[Silence]

Michael: Wassamatta? Laryngitis? Someone put superglue in your cocoa? You hate me?

Pat: We hate you, Michael.

Michael: Whew! Thank the blessed Lord. I thought it might be something serious. Want a drink?

Maureen: We just got one.

Michael: Oh. Well I'll have a Pernod and blackcurrant.

[Pat hesitates, sees that Michael is expecting him to buy a drink for him and gets up reluctantly and exits to the bar]

Maureen: How are ya Michael? Still at Foster's?

Michael: Nah. Gave that up. Didn't like all the chicken's feet on the floor.

Maureen: Chicken's feet?

Michael: Yeah. They cut them off with a kind of bolt cutter.

Maureen: That's nice.

Michael: Killing things is not P.C. Maureen. It's not our right to remove those lonely little things from the pain of living. Why shouldn't they suffer a little longer, like the rest of us?

Maureen: I don't suffer. Not that much.

Michael: Yeah. But at least if it gets too much you can top yourself. A chicken can't do that.

Maureen: [looking bored] No.

[Pat returns with the drink]

Pat: So. Michael. Still at Foster's?

Maureen: He didn't like the chicken's feet.

Pat: On the scrounge, then?

Michael: I've got a new fridge.

Maureen: That's nice. Hotpoint? Ours is a Hotpoint.

Michael: Where's the sense in calling a fridge Hotpoint? Cold point. Freezing point. I could understand that.

Pat: Well. It's been nice to see ya, Michael. We're just....

Michael: I spent the whole morning opening and closing the door. Trying to answer the unanswerable.
[Silence]

Michael: You're curious. You want to know what I mean.

Pat: Michael. We're on our way to....

Michael: What I mean is this. There's a little light in the fridge. Like yours, I expect.

Maureen: It helps to see the food at night I suppose. Saves buying a torch.

Pat: Don't be ridiculous. Why pay 200 for a fridge to save buying a five quid torch?

Maureen: Torches can't keep food fresh.

Pat: We've got a larder.... and a torch.

Maureen: Well. That's all very fine. But what about frozen food?

Pat: Never touch it. We get all our veg from Ainsley's on the coast road.

Maureen: We like frozen. From Bejam's.

Pat: Horses for courses. If you have a picky palate like us, you can't eat frozen. It's like watching someone have a shag, instead of doing it yourself.

Michael: Or like someone getting stuck with a brat instead of you.

Maureen: I want children.

Michael: Well, yes, Sorry, Maureen. It was just a poorly chosen example. I didn't mean...

Maureen: Pat and I are going to have lots, aren't we Pat?

Pat: Yeah.

Michael: Anyhow, The little light in the fridge brings up a very important philosophical question. Concerning epistemology.

Pat: You got any fags, Maur?

Maureen: Yeah. [Rummages in her handbag and hands him a packet]

Pat: Oh not fuckin' fresh air again! Not worth the trouble. I wanted a ciggy and you hand me an oxygen mask!

[Maureen looks at him, takes one out of the packet and lights it]

Michael: So. You know what it is?

Maureen: What is?

Michael: The point I'm making.

Maureen: No, but I'm sure you're going to tell us.

Michael: Right. There's a little button by the hinge. When the door closes, it's supposed to press on it and switch the light off. Saves the element.

Pat: So what?

Michael: I sat by the fridge all morning, just opening and closing that fucking door. Open. Shut. Open. Shut. Know why?

Maureen: [Suddenly slightly interested] No, why?

Michael: Because when the door's closed, I can't KNOW if the light's off.

Pat: Yes you can. You just said about the switch.

Michael: Oh yes, I can SURMISE that the door presses tightly enough to open the circuit. But I can't know. Not for certain. The perceptual experience is denied me. It's an epistemological conundrum.

Pat: It's a heap of shite.

Michael: No. Listen. It's very simple. Reasoning enables me to predict that the light should be off, but I can't VERIFY that prediction.

Pat: Look, Michael, we've got to be...... got to be at..... Shelly's at 7:30, and it's.....

Michael: Look. It's the fuckin' scientific method. Observation, Hypothesis, experiment, result, conclusion. I see a phenomenon and I design an experiment to explain what's going on.

Pat: Take the fridge apart.

Michael: What would that do?

Pat: Just leave the door, the frame and the light. Then you can SEE the light go on and off.

Micheal: That's not the point.

Maureen: What about the warranty?

Pat: Look, Michael. You just fucking said......

Michael: That was a bad example.

Maureen: I'm going to powder my nose.

Pat: You're going for a piss?

Maureen: No, my nose.

Pat: Look, why don't you just say you're going for a piss like any other sane human being? It gets my fucking goat, this powder my nose business. It's just like mum. She always asks people "where's the smallest room in the house?". She seems to forget that our bathroom's bigger than the kitchen. What's she going to do? Crap in the frying pan?

Maureen: Don't be crude. I'm going for a PISS! Alright?
[She goes]

Michael: It's not the point.

Pat: What isn't?

Michael: It's to do with verifying things.

Pat: What?

Michael: All experiential knowledge must be verifiable, or it isn't knowledge at all.

Pat: So, for instance, if I cracked this glass over your skull, you could verify that I'd cracked the glass over your skull and conclude that I'd cracked the fucking glass over your skull?

Michael: That's right.

Pat: It's shite.

Michael: It isn't. Bishop Berkeley didn't think so.

Pat: Is he Catholic?

Michael: It's not important, I mean I think so, but it doesn't.....

Pat: It's all the same God, right?

Michael: He's dead. Centuries ago.

Pat: But you still...

Michael: He was right.

Pat: Believe what you want, Michael.

[Maureen returns]

Maureen: I want some crisps, Pat.

Pat: We'll be for supper soon.

Maureen: [Looking at Michael] Oh will we?

Michael: No no. You go. I can't stop long anyhow. Don't worry about me. Go.

Pat: It's alright. We'll go soon. We've got time. What were you saying about Bishop whatsisname?

Michael: You're not interested.

Pat: No, honestly. We are, aren't we love?

Maureen: Of course.
[Silence]

Pat: So?

Michael: Bishop Berkeley believed the physical world wasn't real.

Pat: Really? That's something. What about that, Maur?

Michael: And things only exist if we can see them.

Maureen: So what's the point? We've got to go soon.

Michael: The point is that when the fridge door is closed, I can't see inside, and so the light, on or off, doesn't really exist anyway. [Suddenly Michael stops talking and starts quietly sobbing]

Maureen: I want some crisps. [She hands pat 50p]

Pat: Cheese and onion? [She nods]

Maureen: How's things with Stella?

[Michael takes some time to answer.]

Michael: Could be better.

Maureen: She at home?

Michael: No. Not tonight.

Maureen: At her mam's?

Michael: No.

Maureen: Swimming, bowling, hen night, skiing in France......

Michael: No.

Maureen: She's gone, hasn't she?

Michael: Yes.

Maureen: Michael, I'm so sorry. When?

Michael: Tuesday before last.

Maureen: Is that why you've been playing with the fridge door?

Michael: Partly.

Maureen: It's like the light, isn't it? You can't see Stella anymore, so she doesn't exist, right?

Michael: Something along those lines.

Maureen: If it's any comfort, in a way you're right. Once the door is closed, the light doesn't really exist. And it doesn't matter anymore whether it's on or off.

Michael: But she still loves me.

Maureen: But it doesn't help to think that, does it? She's not there anymore. She doesn't exist. Now you move on.

Michael: To what? Chicken's feet?

Maureen: She doesn't feel the way you do.

Michael: Why not? She loved me.

Maureen: When it's gone, it's gone.

Michael: But where does it go?

Maureen: It goes nowhere. the light is off.

Michael: You don't know that.

Maureen: But you don't know it's on. You can't. It's what you said.

Michael: You know? I just wound up looking at the closed door.

Maureen: It's closed, Michael..
[Pat returns with the crisps]

Pat: They only had salt and vinegar, but look, Maur, we ought to be off.

Maureen: Let's stay here. Then we'll go up the hill.

Pat: You and me, love?

Maureen: And Michael. The wind'll blow the sweat off him.
[Freeze for a second, then blackout]

www.ingramcontent.com/pod-product-compliance
Lightning Source LLC
Chambersburg PA
CBHW022012160426
43197CB00007B/401
* 9 7 8 0 9 5 5 6 9 1 5 0 8 *